Affiliate Millions

Affiliate Millions

*Make a Fortune Using Search Marketing
on Google and Beyond*

ANTHONY BORELLI

GREG HOLDEN

John Wiley & Sons, Inc.

Published by John Wiley & Sons, Inc., Hoboken, New Jersey.
Published simultaneously in Canada.

Wiley Bicentennial Logo: Richard J. Pacifico

For general information on our other products and services or for technical sup-port, please contact our Customer Care Department within the United States at (800) 762-2974, outside the United States at (317) 572–3993 or fax (317) 572–4002.

Wiley also publishes its books in a variety of electronic formats. Some content that appears in print may not be available in electronic formats. For more information about Wiley products, visit our Web site at www.wiley.com.

Library of Congress Cataloging-in-Publication Data:

Borelli, Anthony, 1969-
Affiliate millions : make a fortune using search marketing on Google and beyond / Anthony Borelli, Greg Holden.
    p. cm.
  Includes index.
  ISBN: 978-0-470-10034-9 (cloth)
    1. Internet marketing.   2. Internet advertising.   3. Internet searching.
4. Google.   5. Web search engines. I. Holden, Greg. II. Title.
HF5415.1265.B67 2007
658.8'72—dc22   2006037906

Printed in the United States of America

10 9 8 7 6 5 4 3 2 1

Thanks to my wife, Robyn, and my children, Joshua, Alyssa, Jacob and Hunter for their patience with me during the writing of Affiliate Millions.

CONTENTS

Introduction

For half my life—fully 18 of my 36 years—I filled out time-sheets, accounting for every minute of my workday to corporations both large and small who valued my time far below my own personal estimations of its worth. Degrees and certifications combined with long hours, hard work, and a can-do attitude produced a decade-long string of stellar performance reviews, but did relatively little to raise the value of my time to these corporations.

Please don't misunderstand me. I was paid a competitive wage, received good benefits, enjoyed comfortable working conditions, and was treated with respect. The only real problem was that a large portion of the fruits of my labor had to be shared with the company's owners. The reason that a corporation exists, after all, is to make money for its stockholders.

Even though it was a fair arrangement, I didn't feel that I was getting the best return on the time and money I was investing. No matter who you are or what you do, self-employment is clearly the best—if not the only—way to maximize your potential. As the sole owner of and investor in your own business, there is no one else to claim a share of your profits (except Uncle Sam, perhaps).

But starting my own business with limited reserves of time and money always seemed a daunting task, so I limited my attempts at self-employment to small, part-time ventures.

Then how did I finally become a millionaire? It was almost by accident, actually, that one of the "small" businesses I thought I had started turned out to be a juggernaut that would rocket my earnings into seven figures.

I was working for a corporate IT giant supporting a much smaller company when I received the news that this struggling smaller company would soon close its doors and that my position supporting it would accordingly be eliminated. Every effort would be made to find another job for me within the company, but nothing was guaranteed. This shattered the false sense of security I had counted as one of the benefits of working for a large corporation.

As luck would have it, a third corporation intervened, taking over the failed company's product and offering me a temporary contract that matched my then-current salary, as well as a retention bonus as an incentive for me to defer my search for permanent employment. More important, I was informed that my new duties would be limited to a small amount of maintenance work, and an expected quick response to any system failures. I was free to do as I pleased with the rest of my time, as long as the system ran smoothly.

I recognized immediately that I now had the opportunity to put to good use a sizable chunk of my on-call time, and I began to consider how best to use this time. A set of specifications began to form in my mind that would eventually lead me into the fields of affiliate advertising and search marketing:

- I needed a business I could manage on my own, without the hassle and expense of hiring other employees.

- I had very little in the way of savings to invest and was not interested in a large amount of borrowing. So I needed a business that would not require a lot of start-up money.
- I expected that I would need to secure a full-time position after my current contract expired. So I needed a business that—once established—would not demand a lot of time from me.

Direct marketing appealed to me initially because it was a proven model that would not involve a storefront presence or any inventory. But the problem was that managing the order fulfillment process was clearly a time-consuming component of any successful direct marketing enterprise.

Then a recently failed shopping portal web site I had once managed provided the answer. I had learned about affiliate marketing programs while researching potential advertising revenue sources for this site. I found it was surprisingly easy to join these affiliate programs, and hundreds accepted my affiliate applications before the web site was even fully developed. I also discovered that it was fairly inexpensive and easy to generate traffic to my site using Google's AdWords program to run targeted text ads for my site. The site itself, however, never managed to coax enough of its visitors into continuing on to the affiliate program sites, and so it failed.

As I pondered all this, I had an epiphany of sorts. Why not take a direct marketing approach to affiliate marketing and have my targeted ads send traffic directly to my clients rather than to a web site of my own? I would lower my overhead and shorten the trip to the point of sale. Plus I would save all that time I had previously spent maintaining and updating a web site of my own. Some quick research indicated that I was way behind the curve on this idea and that countless thousands were already using

Google and other search engines to do exactly that. Yet I thought I might be able to carve out a niche for myself that could eventually yield as much as a few hundred dollars a month. I anticipated that there would be little time and effort required to maintain it once I returned to full employment. And so I resolved to give affiliate marketing a try, using Google AdWords' paid search model for marketing these programs.

My goals for the business were exceeded within a few months, and I began to cash checks for hundreds of dollars in commissions. To my great surprise—and delight—the business continued to grow, and the monthly checks soon topped $1,000. By the time my temporary contract expired in June, my monthly income was in the tens of thousands of dollars. Despite working an average of two hours a day, I was earning more than I had ever dreamed possible. Needless to say, I did not apply for another day job. As the year wore on, my modest efforts to grow the business continued to pay huge dividends. In fact, my monthly checks soon broke into six-figure territory, reaching as high as $255,000 in a single month. By the end of the year, my new business had yielded just over $1 million. I was, I realized, an Affiliate Millionaire.

The change this has made in my life is incredible. At the time I write this, I spend all my time at home with my family. Most days require barely an hour or two of work. I have paid off my credit card debts, my car loans, and my mortgage. I'm considering the purchase of a 58-acre horse ranch in Florida.

How did this happen? With so much competition and so little seed money, how did I make a cool million dollars in my first full year of operations? The answer, I now realize, was my multifaceted approach. The competition, it seems, did not fully grasp the multidimensional aspects of affiliate marketing and the new paid search model (introduced by Google AdWords), not to mention how best to maximize potential returns.

My first instinct, as you can imagine, was to keep my story to myself, hoping that months or even years might pass before my secrets would be discovered. Upon further reflection, however, I realized an even bigger opportunity existed. With countless others seeking the path to success that I had already found, marketing my strategy would prove much more rewarding than hoarding information that others would eventually discover on their own.

And so I offer this manual in the hope that my knowledge and experience can launch many others on their way to the financial freedom and independence that I now enjoy. You, dear reader, have my very best wishes as you pursue an American dream—a dream of one day becoming an Affiliate Millionaire.

About the Authors

Anthony Borelli made the move from corporate employee to self-employed affiliate marketer in late 2004. He was initially attracted to this form of online business, which involves the placement of ads on behalf of online businesses such as Amazon, eBay, and Barnes & Noble, because it requires very little in start-up costs and offers the added advantage of working with already established, successful e-businesses.

He joined several companies' affiliate programs and immediately began paying for and placing ads on their behalf with Google and other well-traveled search engines. By carefully selecting the right keywords, judiciously placing bids on these keywords, and tailoring his ads to induce results, he began to make thousands, and eventually tens of thousands, of dollars each month in resulting commissions. (His highest monthly check from affiliate advertising: $255,000.) In his first full year of business, he made over $1 million on Google as a search marketer and affiliate advertiser. He has acquired vast experience in composing ads, evaluating results, and maximizing profits, and he is eager to lead other entrepreneurs to the same kind of success.

Greg Holden is the author of more than 30 books on computers and the Internet. He specializes in books about online business and e-commerce. Virtually all of his books provide both entrepreneurs and small businesses, respectively, with the knowledge and tools they need to expand their operations to include the Internet. Recent titles include *How to Do Everything with Your eBay Business* (Osborne-McGraw Hill), *Secrets of the eBay Millionaires* (Osborne-McGraw Hill), *eBay PowerSellers' Bible* (Wiley), and *Starting an Online Business for Dummies* (Wiley). He is also an active PowerSeller on eBay.

Part I

Getting Started

Chapter 1

How to Make Millions on Google and Other Search Engines: My 10-Step Approach

"**W**hat do you do?" People always ask that question when they first meet you. If you were to turn a movie camera on me and watch me as I go through a typical workday, it probably wouldn't seem like I'm doing much of *anything*, and that's just the way I like it. When I was first learning how to make money placing affiliate ads on Google and other search and content networks, I typically put in a solid eight-hour day, but now that I have the system up and running, things go much easier.

I have turned off the alarm that used to wake me up at 5 a.m. every morning. I sleep as late as I want, unless I take a turn driving my kids to school. Before I became an Affiliate Advertiser, I used to have a 90-minute commute to my job in Greater Boston. Now, all of my commuting time is spent on my pillow. I am my own boss and—I don't mind telling you—I am very easy to work for.

A typical morning now might find me rolling out of bed around eight or nine o'clock and stumbling over to the computer in my bedroom. I check the ad campaigns I have running on sites like Google and MSN adCenter. My formal performance-monitoring routine takes about an hour, but most mornings I simply perform a quick check on four things (don't worry if these terms don't make any sense to you right now; I'll explain them later):

1. *The click-through rate (CTR).* I make sure the percentage of people who are clicking through the ads I place and going to the advertisers' web sites are broadly in the range I expect for the day of the week or the time of day.
2. *Volume.* I check to see whether the volume of traffic is roughly what I expect it to be at that time.
3. *Cost per click.* I make certain the cost per click for each of my campaigns is in the range I have come to expect for the day of the week or the time of day.
4. *Commissions.* I make certain that my commissions from the day before are roughly what I would expect for the traffic generated.

Most days, everything is working exactly as it should be. On these fine mornings, I may simply go back to sleep, or I may go downstairs to enjoy a leisurely breakfast. Just as often, I might give my wife a break by taking the kids to school so she won't have to. Whenever I happen to feel the most motivated, I will usually spend an hour (or even two) doing some basic monitoring and performance-tuning tasks. On rare days, I might spend hours or a whole day trying to start a new campaign in a particularly competitive advertising space, but most days I do very little real work. In exchange for these "burdensome" tasks, I regularly receive checks of over $100,000 per month in my mailbox (okay, now that I've learned how to have them deposited directly into my checking account, they don't show up in my mailbox anymore, but you get the point). I bought a beautiful new home in Florida with cash, and my family and I enjoy regular vacations wherever we like.

A LITTLE HISTORY

I'm not telling you my personal story because I especially like to talk about myself or because I'm boasting. I am telling you this because, when you know a little bit more about me, you'll realize that anyone, including yourself, can become a successful entrepreneur through paid search marketing and affiliate advertising.

As I mentioned in my introduction, I have managed some small web sites, but the few web sites I created never made much money, and maintaining them never appealed to me that much. This might seem surprising, because the best-known traditional model to make money through affiliate advertising is as follows:

- Create a content web site and publicize it in order to attract as many visitors as possible.
- Take advantage of the established traffic by placing text and banner affiliate ads that turn the site into a source of revenue.

I did assemble a couple of web sites that attempted to make money this way. They generated small amounts of revenue here and there, but the cost of driving traffic to my site exceeded the modest revenues I was able to generate. You see, very few of the visitors I paid for actually clicked on any of the ads on my own site. They had already clicked on an ad for my site, after all, and most were not willing to click through to yet another ad.

Why Send Anyone to My Own Site First?

Since I was having such a difficult time converting the traffic I generated from running ads for my web site on search and content networks like Google, the question eventually occurred to me, "Why not place the affiliate ads directly on Google instead?"

At the time, I thought the idea of placing affiliate ads on a search engine site was a great epiphany of my own. Since then, I've discovered that I wasn't the first to come up with this idea—not by a long shot—but I may be one of the most successful. Initially, the idea appealed to me because it required no overhead, no inventory, and it seemed like something I could do in the spare hour or two I would have each day after I went back to full-time employment (which I was planning to do before long). Remember, my initial goal was to bring in only an extra $200 or $300 a month. I didn't realize in the beginning that this could be my ticket to financial freedom.

Bitten by the Bug

At first, I signed up with a few affiliate programs and started placing ads for a small number of products. I began by losing a small amount of money—several cents per click. I adjusted the margins a bit, and I discovered a few products on which I could make a few dollars each day. Then, I made a couple of very expensive mistakes that cost me several thousand dollars in the space of just a few hours. Believe it or not, I almost gave up entirely and completely missed out on the fortune I eventually would make. A few thousand dollars was an enormous amount of money to me at that time, and if this was the kind of risk I would be taking, I reasoned, what chance did I have of making that kind of money back? For nearly a week, I swore off the entire idea.

Then I thought about it and decided to give it another try. After all, I had already found a couple of products on which I could make a few dollars a day, so why not at least leave those campaigns running?

Then the bug bit me: "If you can make money advertising these products, you can find other products that will make even more." Of course, I proceeded much more carefully (as I will teach you to do) and avoided taking unnecessary risks on unproven campaigns. After putting together several campaigns that provided me with modest returns, I made my first big breakthrough. In December of 2004, I hit on one advertising campaign that generated more than $7,000, which was well beyond my wildest dreams for the business at that time. This success lit a fire under me, and I set out to find other products and programs that would turn out to be big winners.

I resolved to tap into untapped market niches and to aggressively pursue establishing campaigns in competitive market spaces as well. My initial hard work paid off, and one by one I added established, successful campaigns to my portfolio, some of which brought in just a few dollars a day, while others made hundreds or even thousands. All these campaigns, meanwhile, required very little maintenance once they were up and running. I soon found myself spending less and less effort on the risky and time-consuming process of establishing new campaigns, and my focus shifted to the increasingly rewarding practice of monitoring and fine-tuning my existing campaigns.

Before long—even though I was now working an average of just two hours a day—I was earning more than I had ever thought possible. My monthly advertising revenue checks broke into six-figure territory and, needless to say, I never went back to my day job.

MY 10 STEPS TO BECOMING AN AFFILIATE MILLIONAIRE

The steps required to become a successful search marketer and affiliate advertiser are well within the reach of anyone, regardless of prior business experience. The building blocks you need to construct your new search marketing–based business are already online and waiting for you to take advantage of them. All you need is a bit of time, a computer connected to the Internet, and a little good advice.

Bookstore shelves are lined with dozens of volumes that promise to teach you how to go online and start your own business or open up a new revenue stream, but few offer you the potential that *Affiliate Millions* does. Books can take you only so far, however. It's up to you to take the first step. In fact, any process goes more easily if you break it into a series of discrete steps—tasks that you can tackle one at a time. In this section, you get a step-by-step overview of the entire process of becoming a successful search marketer, advertising a variety of affiliate programs on Google and other search and content networks.

Step 1. Set Your Sights on Success

I didn't start to make serious money until I had a modest amount of success on which to base my efforts. Then my imagination kicked in and I began to envision just how much money I could make if I stepped up my efforts. I'm asking you to begin by expanding your imagination and believing that you can be a success. In many ways, becoming a successful online entrepreneur is a matter of your mind-set and your attitude.

Step 2. Learn about Affiliate Advertising

In Chapter 2, I introduce you to the concept of affiliate advertising in detail. Affiliate advertising is the revenue side of this whole process, so pay close attention. Once you have a handle on the concept of affiliate advertising, I introduce you to the second half of the equation: search marketing.

Step 3. Learn about Search Marketing

Search marketing is the process by which we drive traffic to the affiliate programs we promote. Chapter 3 introduces you to this concept and helps you understand just how you can use search marketing, instead of a web site of your own, to make affiliate advertising more profitable for you than you might ever have imagined.

Step 4. Join an Affiliate Network

Once you have identified your goals and done some initial thinking about the kinds of products you want to promote, you need to join an affiliate network. An *affiliate network* is a company that works with many different companies to manage and/or promote its affiliate programs and to track the number of clicks, commissions, and so forth that individual affiliates generate for the programs. These networks offer these affiliate programs to publishers and search marketers, giving them a central location to search for appropriate ad copy, consolidating commission checks, and guaranteeing accurate accounting of click traffic and commissions. Affiliate networks are indispensable resources; in Chapter 4, I introduce you to some and walk you step-by-step through the process of joining a few of them.

Step 5. Join Affiliate Programs

Once you have been accepted into one or more affiliate networks, you can start joining the affiliate programs you want to promote. In Chapter 5, I tell you what to look for in an affiliate program, and then I walk you through the process of joining some programs, taking you all the way to generating the tracking code you will need to set up your ads in the next step.

Step 6. Create Search Marketing Campaigns

Signing up with an affiliate network is only one piece of the puzzle. You also need to join one or more search and content networks on which to run your affiliate ads. Google AdWords is an excellent place to start. In Chapter 6, I show you how to join Google and other search and content networks, and I take you step-by-step through the process of creating your first ad campaign.

Step 7. Learn How to Manage Your Search Campaigns

Just getting your campaigns running isn't the end of the process. Not by a long shot. You'll need to learn how to evaluate your ad campaigns and monitor and improve them as well. Chapter 7 shows you how to use the reporting features you'll need to be familiar with—a simple process, by the way—and Chapter 9 teaches you how to monitor those results and improve existing campaigns.

Step 8. Don't Let Mistakes Get You Down

Every entrepreneur encounters problems early on, and most make mistakes from time to time. What separates those who go on to success from the ones who crash and burn? The winners learn from their mistakes and don't let setbacks deter them. In Chapter 10, I talk about some common, but sometimes costly, mistakes that I have made: what to watch for, how to catch mistakes early, and how to recover from those mistakes.

Step 9. Invest and Grow Your Ad Programs

Businesspeople who sell tangible products know that you have to plan ahead. You have to order in advance and assemble more of an inventory than you actually need in order to grow and prosper. In this business, your only inventory is your cash on hand, but you still need to manage it as if it were a product on the shelves. After all, the ads you pay to run comprise your product, and you need to budget carefully to ensure you can keep that product available every day.

In Chapter 11, I talk about growing your business by searching for profitable new campaigns and by expanding successful existing ones, too. The sky is the limit, as they say, and if you keep pushing the limit, there's no telling how far you'll go.

Step 10. Manage Your Business Like a Business

Running your own business and being your own boss is fantastic, believe me, but it isn't always easy. You'll need to pay taxes on your profits, remember, and if you reach a certain level of success, you may find it necessary to hire an accountant and even a lawyer.

Chapter 12 addresses a number of these concerns and gets you thinking about some of the duller, but nonetheless important, aspects of running your own business.

MY MESSAGE TO YOU: HAVE FAITH IN YOURSELF

If you have a positive frame of mind, a good work ethic, and just a little intelligence you can market just about anything. If you plan ahead and stick with your marketing efforts for the long haul, you *will* be successful.

Making money online is a leap of faith for most people. To the overwhelming majority of the general public, the idea of selling tangible goods or services online is like learning an obscure foreign language. When you consider that in the case of affiliate marketing your product is a digital ad on a Web page, it can be an even bigger leap of faith. Take it step-by-step and read the chapters that follow, and you'll stand a good chance of becoming an Affiliate Millionaire yourself.

Chapter 2

Learning about Affiliate Advertising

Affiliate advertising (sometimes also referred to as *affiliate marketing*) is the term currently used to describe one type of program a web site typically sets up to allow other sites to advertise their products and/or services and to receive commissions in return. Such programs are often open to almost anyone with a web site, newsletter, or other electronic means of running the affiliate program's ads. Typically, the web site either creates an affiliate program Web page on its own site or contracts with an affiliate network to promote and run its affiliate program. Either way, companies that create such programs develop various types of text and image advertisements, embed them with special tracking codes that allow them to know who sent them the traffic, and encourage affiliates to use these advertisements to promote their sites.

GETTING UP TO SPEED

Affiliate advertising is one of those concepts that can seem a bit overwhelming, even after you have tried it for a while. The way to grasp the whole subject is to break it into components. Affiliate advertising can be best understood by defining its three basic components: affiliates, affiliate programs, and affiliate networks. Once you have a basic understanding of these elements, you'll be able to start signing up for programs and creating your first accounts.

Who Are the Affiliates?

You are. Affiliates are entrepreneurs like yourself who are willing to advertise other web sites' products and services for a commission. These affiliate commissions may be only a secondary revenue stream for some entrepreneurs whose primary online business is complemented by running relevant ads on some pages. For others, it may represent their primary revenue stream. Affiliates can use one of several models to conduct their affiliate advertising activities.

Personal and Business Web Sites. Traditionally, affiliate marketers have placed advertisements on web sites they create themselves. These web sites may provide a product or service of their own, running a few ads in appropriate locations to create a little extra revenue. In some cases these web sites might contain some type of content (news, blogs, etc.) to attract visitors, while relying entirely on advertisements to generate revenue. In either case, the key to the success of their affiliate advertising revenue stream is the ability not just to drive traffic to their site, but also to provide advertisements relevant to the content of the site that their visitors are likely to find inviting.

One of the most commonly seen types of ads today is not a traditional banner ad, but a dynamically generated ad that relates in some way to the Web page content near it. For instance, if you create a Web page about science and astronomy, or if you simply make a passing mention of telescopes in your blog, you can place an advertising code provided by Google AdSense on the page and it will dynamically serve up a mixture of ads, all related to your site—in this case, astronomy. Some examples of sample ads related to telescopes are shown in Figure 2.1.

E-publications. Regular publications such as newsletters that are e-mailed to subscribers are effective ways to reach customers who have "opted in" to what you have to say by signing up. As there is no cost associated with sending an e-mail message beyond the time and effort put into writing it, these e-publications can be cost effective—once you have built up a sizable list of subscribers, that is. Newsletters can take time to prepare, and attracting and retaining subscribers can be a very tricky task. E-publications sent to active subscribers should not be confused with unwanted and

Figure 2.1 Traditional Ads by Affiliates and Other Marketers Are Placed on Web Pages
Source: Screenshots © Google Inc. and are used with permission.

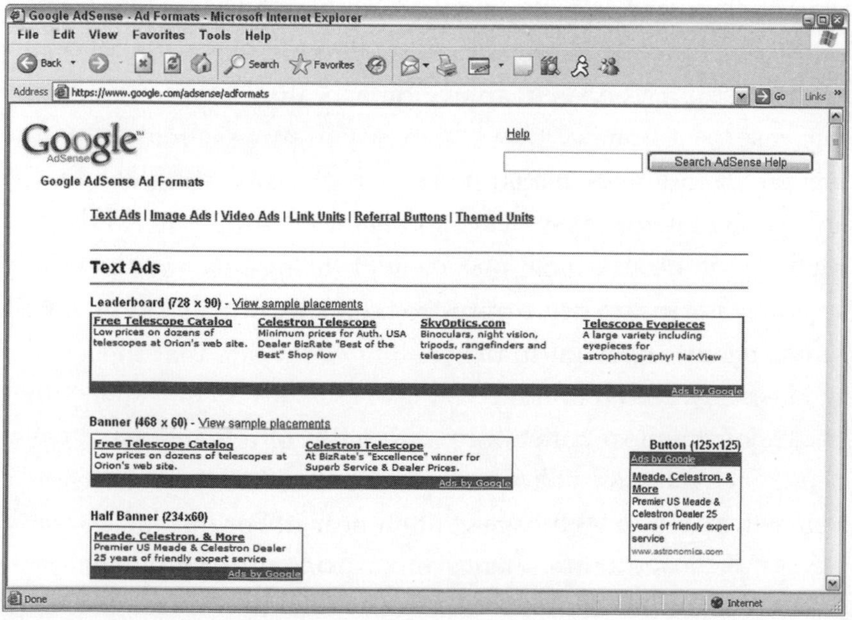

unrequested junk e-mail. You should mail e-publications and newsletters only to users who request to be added as regular subscribers to the publication.

Free Software or Freeware. An excellent source of revenue can be embedded affiliate ads in helpful programs that Web surfers can download for free. A *freeware* program, which performs a service the user wants and needs, makes it clear that downloading the product will result in the display of occasional advertisements so that the service can remain free. This should not be confused with the unscrupulous practice of embedding *spyware*, which may install itself uninvited or which may not explain the commercial aspects of software before it is downloaded.

Search Marketing. My preferred method of advertising, and the only advertising method that will be covered in detail in this book, is search marketing. Or, to be more specific, paid search marketing on a variety of paid search and content networks. *Paid search* refers to the practice of charging for the placement of ads in search results or on specific content-related web sites (remember AdSense?)—a practice that makes search and content networks lots of money. Most search marketers place ads on paid search and content networks such as Google, Yahoo!, and MSN. On MSN, as on other search and content networks, these paid ads appear both at the top and on the right-hand side of a page of search results (see Figure 2.2).

These paid search advertisements are my bread and butter, and using them to generate wealth is the primary focus of this book. I have made millions of dollars already, and if you apply yourself, you just might make a few million yourself. Chapter 3 offers more information about search engines and paid search ads.

Figure 2.2   Search Marketers Use the Visibility of Search and Content Networks Like This to Place Affiliate Ads
Source: Microsoft product screen shot reprinted with permission from Microsoft Corporation.

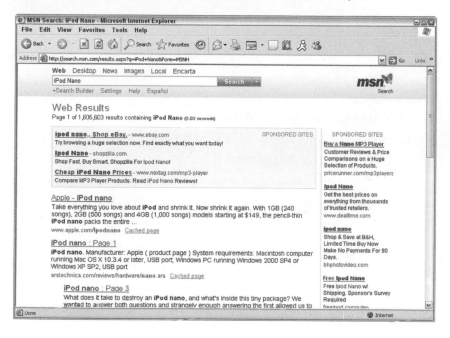

What Are Affiliate Programs?

An affiliate program is a vehicle for web sites that allows them to offer commissions to affiliates for the clicks/leads/sales they generate on behalf of that company. The program may be geared toward selling products, registering new users, generating sales leads, or collecting consumer information. Whatever the goal, affiliates are encouraged to join these programs and drive relevant traffic to the affiliate program's web site.

What Are Affiliate Networks?

An affiliate network doesn't place ads for companies. It is a company that functions as a sort of go-between, providing services

the merchants who have products to advertise and the
who advertise them. Affiliate networks offer lots of
important value-added services, such as tracking clicks, visits,
purchases, and other actions; providing tools for reporting how
many people view an ad, or click on it; and processing payments
to affiliates. They also help bring affiliates together with advertisers: Advertisers might have to pay a fee to join the network, but
they are able to provide the network with logos and other advertising materials, and the network helps by publicizing them to
their individual affiliate members.

You might hear the word *tier* used in conjunction with affiliate
networks. Some networks are two-tier, some are three-tier, and so
on. A tier is a step on a system of sign-ups: If you are a member of
a network and you sign up someone else to make a purchase, you
are said to be on the first tier, and the person who signed up is on
the second tier. You earn a referral fee for signing up the second-
tier member. The second-tier member, in turn, can earn a referral
fee for signing up someone else, but only if the network allows
that number of tiers. Some of the best-known affiliate networks
are listed here (this brief list is just a sampling, not a comprehensive survey, of affiliate networks):

> **Commission Junction / BFAST (www.cj.com).** Commis-
> sion Junction is one of the largest, if not *the* largest, payment
> network for advertising and e-commerce traffic. You'll find
> out more about how to use it later in this chapter.

> **Affiliate Fuel (www.affiliatefuel.com).** This highly re-
> garded affiliate network offers a variety of tools and re-
> porting options that can be extremely valuable to search
> marketers. Affiliate Fuel is particularly active in educa-
> tional affiliate programs and offers some of the highest
> commissions and conversion rates in that industry.

Advertising.com (www.advertising.com). This advertising network primarily uses a pay-per-click model. The network tracks the placement of banner ads on web sites. Advertising.com is notable for its "intelligent modeling system," which keeps track of the types of ads that have attracted the greatest response on your site. The system then places similar ads on the site.

LinkShare (www.linkshare.com). A pioneer of online affiliate marketing that advertises itself as the largest pay-for-performance affiliate marketing network on the Internet.

Performics (www.performics.com). This performance-based marketing division of DoubleClick bills itself as an online marketing service for leading multichannel marketers.

eAdvertising (www.eadvertising.com). This subsidiary of LeadClick Media advertises itself as a "private CPA network." Publishers can use banners, pop-ups, and search ads.

Commission Structures

As a search marketer, your main goal is to get paid for placing ads. The advertisers who agree to let you place ads don't have a problem with paying you. They do, however, have different payment systems.

Pay Per Click. A pay-per-click commission structure pays you a fixed amount—generally between 3 and 25 cents per click—for each click (or visitor) you send to the client's web site. Most pay-per-click commission programs specifically prohibit search marketing, however, so you would take advantage of these types of

is only if you had a content site of your own on which to
e.

Pay Per Sale. Pay-per-sale programs fall into two categories:

1. *Percentage of sale or revenue.* You receive a percentage of the
   purchase price or a percentage of revenue (net profit).
2. *Fixed commission per sale.* Instead of a percentage of the
   sale price, you receive a fixed commission (e.g., $5 or $10
   per sale).

You might hear one of these options called *revenue sharing*.
Some affiliate programs give you the option of choosing a percentage or fixed commission. A commission can range between 5
and 60 percent of the purchase price, so examine the eventual
purchase prices of the items you are going to promote: You might
actually do better with a flat commission.

Pay Per Lead/Action. Information is the coin of the realm for
many web sites. These sites place as much value in receiving
someone's contact information and having them fill out a form or
download a piece of software as they do in purchasing a tangible
good or service. They pay affiliates when someone clicks on their
ad and performs a particular action. Some examples include:

- *Completes forms.* Such sites pay a fee when someone you
  refer fills out a form. Typically, a form requires the person
  to submit a name, address, and e-mail address, all of which
  can be used for subsequent marketing contacts.
- *Opts for free registrations.* Sites like the auction giant eBay
  (www.ebay.com) will pay affiliates if a click on one of their
  ads causes the clicker to sign up with eBay, although they

do require that the newly registered user become an active user by placing at least one bid or purchasing or listing at least one item.

- *Takes advantage of free downloads.* Some sites will pay you a referral fee if a click on one of your ads leads to a download of software they provide. Downloads can lead to eventual purchases of the software.

Sites that don't sell tangible goods and services but that develop computer software or provide information that you have to register to use are good candidates for affiliate programs. Look for sites that are especially popular and that are relatively new—in other words, those that don't already have millions of registered users that are still growing steadily.

In my opinion, pay-per-lead/action programs tend to be the most profitable ones for search marketers. In general, the less a program wants you to get the customer to do or to spend, the easier it will be for you to find customers who will perform the actions you need to receive a fee.

NOTE: You might see pay-per-lead/action programs referred to as cost per action (CPA) by some affiliate programs.

Mixed Payment Systems. Some sites, like eBay, have well-developed affiliate systems that pay differently for different actions. First, if you place an ad that causes someone to register with eBay for the first time and then use his or her new registration to place a bid, you earn a fee of between $12 and $22. At the same time, eBay operates a revenue-sharing program in which affiliates earn a percentage of the revenue eBay generates from each sale—not of the final sale price—when they refer someone who places a winning bid or makes an instant "Buy It Now" purchase.

Each aspect of eBay's commission structure requires that, in order to be paid, the shoppers have to actually be willing to spend money—they have to place a bid if they are new registrants or place a winning bid or make a purchase if they are currently an eBay member. Because of the need to attract shoppers who must actually follow through in some way, eBay can be a difficult market to crack: It's difficult to write ads that prompt the correct actions, and it's also difficult to fine-tune and manage advertising programs. Not only that, but eBay's popularity makes the competition particularly fierce. Nevertheless, because eBay is such a vast marketplace, the advertising opportunities are virtually endless. To find out more about eBay's options for affiliates, visit http://affiliates.ebay.com.

HOW DO I GET STARTED?

Naturally, by now you are anxious to get started, and you are probably wondering when we can begin joining affiliate programs and start earning money. Don't worry, we'll get there soon, but first we need to introduce you to one more concept. Remember when we discussed the different models that affiliates use to promote the affiliate programs they join? I identified search marketing as my preferred method of advertising these programs. Search marketing is the tool you will use to make your affiliate advertising business a real success, so you need to understand this concept as well before you can really get started. In Chapter 3, you'll learn more about search marketing, the difference between *paid* and *natural* search, and the distinctions between *search networks* and *content networks*.

Chapter 3

Learning about Search Marketing

There are lots of ways to make money online with affiliate advertising, but one method requires less time, less money, and less computer know-how than all the others, and that method is search marketing. Search marketing with Google and other search and content networks is the model that's been most successful for me. As you'll see in later chapters, it's also an advertising medium over which I can exercise a great deal of fine-grained control. I turned to search marketing on search and content networks like Google specifically because I didn't want the upkeep and overhead required to maintain a web site of my own. I had no idea that in addition to being the easiest and most efficient way to earn money as an affiliate advertiser, it could also be the most profitable.

In this chapter you will learn about search marketers and search marketing. You will find out just what a search and content network is and identify some of the major networks available today. You will also learn the difference between the search and content sides of these networks and how to run your ads on one or the other or both. Finally, I point out some of the reasons why search marketing is the promotional method of choice when it comes to affiliate advertising.

23

WHO ARE SEARCH MARKETERS?

Who are search marketers? Very soon now, *you* will be. For the most part, search marketers are enterprising individuals who know something about how the Web works and who have faith in the power of search engines to attract lots of visitors who want to find particular facts and figures online.

Sometimes, search marketers are people who have been employed in a field like Web design, web site management, or search engine optimization. They find themselves "between jobs" or with extra time on their hands, and they turn to search marketing almost as an experiment, to see how far they can go with it. Other people with little or no prior experience, like myself, stumble across it somehow and discover an unknown and innate talent for marketing and, with the limitless potential of the Internet, they quickly parlay that talent into a fortune.

Of course, search marketing is not for everybody. Some people have asked me for advice about search marketing, have taken out a few ads, and have quickly folded their cards when they lost some money. They didn't have the patience and the drive to stay with search marketing, and the lack of instant success was enough to make them give up. If you don't possess some degree of patience—and a little bit of intelligence—then your search marketing career is likely to be short and expensive.

> **TIP:** Some search marketers like Todd Mintz and knowledgeable writers like Jennifer Laycock contribute to the Search Engine Marketing section of the Search Engine Guide web site (www.searchengineguide .com). Their contributions to the site can tell you more about who search marketers are and what they want from advertisers.

WHAT IS SEARCH MARKETING?

Search marketing, also sometimes referred to as *search engine marketing* or *paid search marketing*, is a collection of marketing methods used to increase the visibility of a web site in the search engine results pages of one or more search and content networks. There are two basic types of search results: *natural search results* and *sponsored search results*. Sponsored search results are your primary concern here, but I will give a brief description of both.

Natural Search

Natural search results are, quite simply, a list of web sites, descriptions, and links to the sites in question. These are returned in response to the keywords entered into the search engine, which are used in an algorithm to select these sites from the search engine's index of sites. Figure 3.1 highlights the natural search results on Google for the search term *computer jobs*.

Notice that the natural search results do not always start immediately. Sometimes, sponsored search ads will appear above the natural search results, seemingly almost as part of the natural search results. You'll learn more about sponsored search soon enough, though. For now, let's get back to natural search. There are two ways to promote a site in the natural search results: search engine optimization (SEO) and paid inclusion.

1. *Search engine optimization (SEO).* Search engine optimization is the process by which you attempt to improve a web site's rankings for relevant keywords in search results by optimizing the web site structure and content in such a way as to make it more easily read and cataloged by the search engine's software. The goal is to have the optimized site recognized by the search engine's software

Figure 3.1   Google's Natural Search Results
Source: Screenshots © Google Inc. and are used with permission.

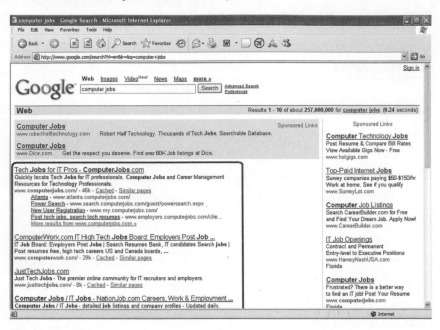

as more relevant than other sites and to appear higher up in the search result listings as a result of the optimization. Traffic generated by natural search results does not have to cost the site owner anything, so the search engine optimization process can make a tremendous difference in a site's overall success and profitability.

2. *Paid inclusion.* Paid inclusion involves paying a search engine or search network to include a web site in its natural search index rather than simply submitting the site for consideration and possible inclusion for free. A site might also pay for a guaranteed high ranking in the natural search results.

That is as much as you need to know about natural search for now. The real focus of this chapter is sponsored search.

Sponsored Search

Sponsored, or paid, search results are actually advertisements— usually text—triggered by the same keywords that search engines use to select web sites for their natural search results. These text advertisements run to the right side of the natural search results and sometimes just above them. These ads are usually identified as sponsored results, but because of the performance algorithms used by the premiere search engines, these paid advertisements are also highly relevant to the search terms entered, and many users are quite willing to click on these ads if they appear to offer what they are searching for. Figure 3.2 highlights these sponsored ads as they appear at the top and right side of Google's search results.

Figure 3.2 Sponsored Ads on Google
Source: Screenshots © Google Inc. and are used with permission.

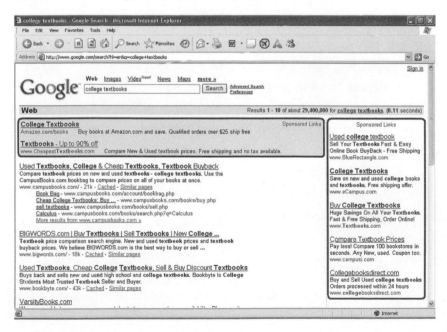

The format is similar on most other search engines as well. Figures 3.3 and 3.4 show the same search results and ad placements on MSN and Yahoo!

Regardless of where these ads actually appear, however, there are two basic models for sponsored search: pay for placement and performance-based paid search. Although both models can be used to make money in affiliate advertising, the performance-based model offers greater opportunities to affiliate advertisers who rely on search marketing to generate their affiliate commissions.

Pay for Placement. The pay-for-placement model simply rewards the highest bidders with the highest ad placements, which usually generate the highest volume of clicks. This can be an excellent

Figure 3.3 Sponsored Ads on MSN
Source: Microsoft product screen shot reprinted with permission from Microsoft Corporation.

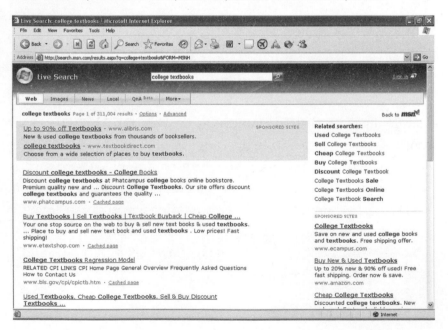

Figure 3.4 Sponsored Ads on Yahoo!
Source: Reproduced with permission of Yahoo! Inc. © 2006 by Yahoo! Inc. YAHOO! and the YAHOO! logo are trademarks of Yahoo! Inc.

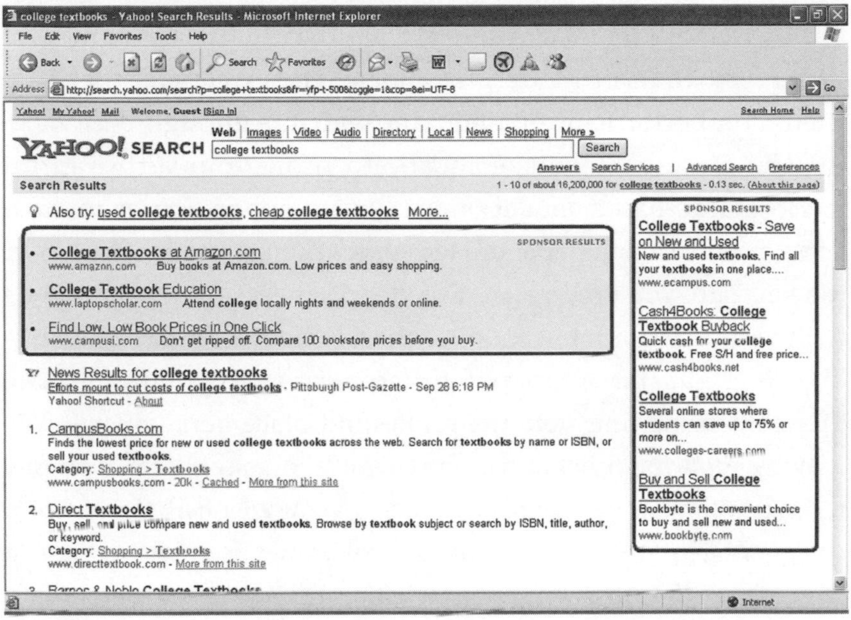

option for a Web business that has higher margins than its competitors and can afford to pay more and still make a profit, but it is a very difficult model for affiliate advertisers to make profitable. The reason for this difficulty is that affiliates are often competing with dozens, hundreds, or even thousands of other affiliates trying to promote the same affiliate programs using the same keywords. Naturally, the return on any given keyword is roughly the same for all affiliates marketing the same program, and typically a number of them are bidding just under or right up to the amount they all know they will earn, on average, per click. This leaves a very narrow margin, if any, on which to build a profit.

There are a couple of ways to overcome this difficulty. For affiliate programs that offer performance tiers (higher payments for delivering more customers), an affiliate could aggressively attempt to outbid his or her competitors across a large number of relevant keywords and phrases with the goal of reaching one of the top performance tiers and thus raising the return per click above most of the competition. I discuss performance tiers in greater detail in Chapter 9, "Performance Monitoring and Tuning."

The second method would be to tailor your ad to attract fewer, *but more relevant,* clicks than the other ads. For instance, if your commission is dependent on users *paying to register* in order to use a site, you could state this clearly in the ad. Fewer people will click on the ad, but more of those who do click on the ad—knowing that they must pay to register—will actually register, therefore providing you with a commission. You will now be making more per click, on average, and be able to afford to pay more per click, thus raising your ad to a higher position, where it can generate more volume. You'll learn more about writing ads in the coming chapters, but for now let's get back to learning about search marketing options.

Performance-Based Paid Search. The performance-based search engine algorithms are really your best bet for setting yourself apart from the competition and making real money. Here is how they work: Instead of giving the highest placement to the highest bidder, a performance-based algorithm also looks at the click-through rate (CTR) of each ad. If one ad has a higher CTR than another ad, the ad with the higher CTR will not have to bid as much as the lower-performing ad to run above it. How much less you may be required to bid and still run above the higher-paying ad depends on just how much higher your CTR is compared to the competing ad or ads. If your CTR is more than double that of the other ads, you might bid and pay as little as half as much and still have your ad run above the competition, generating more clicks at a lower cost than your competition. That's right—more clic\ lower cost. So remember to pay attention later, when you\ learning how to write these ads, because ad copy is *king* in the land of performance-based search marketing!

WHAT ARE SEARCH AND CONTENT NETWORKS?

Search and content networks are arguably the most flexible and relevant advertising vehicles in existence, and a modern-day gold rush has quietly been building up steam around them for a decade or more. By allowing you to pick keywords and phrases to trigger your ads, you control who sees these ads with a level of detail never before possible. Unlike in the old days, though, this modern-day gold rush doesn't require that you pick up and leave everything else behind while you seek your fortune in some far-away land. In fact, you need not even quit your day job.

As I mentioned before, there are two basic types of search and content networks: pay for placement and performance-based. The pay-for-placement model is the traditional one. Explained quite simply, the highest bidder receives the highest ad position in relation to search results and pays the most per click for that privilege. This model may serve some businesses well, but for a search marketer and affiliate advertiser who often competes against many other search marketers advertising the same affili-ate programs, there is little or no money to be made. The earnings per click will be virtually the same for anyone bidding on the same keyword and advertising the same affiliate program, and the result is usually several ads bidding right up to the maximum amount you are likely to be able to earn per click. There are some exceptions, to be sure, but I largely avoid these types of search engines, as there is little hope of making a decent return on my investment of time and money.

The newer, performance-based search and content networks are your best bet. Rather than giving the highest position to the person willing to pay the most, performance-based algorithms take into account the actual performance of your ad in relation to others. If your ad is clicked on 10 percent of the times it is viewed, and your competitor's ad is clicked on only 5 percent of the time, these algorithms recognize that the search engine can make more money running your ad even by charging you just a little more than half of what your competitor might be willing to pay. That's right, you can get a higher position (which translates directly to higher volume) for a lower cost if you write an ad that outperforms the competition. If you forget everything else I tell you, remember this: Ad copy is *king*!

Numerous search and content networks are available online; for a more complete and up-to-date list, you can visit www .AffiliateMillions.com, but for now I list just a few of the big ones.

First-Tier Search and Content Networks

These networks are among the largest and best-known search engines, and sometimes lesser-known search pages are powered behind the scenes by these engines and their search algorithms. More important, however, these search engines provide high-quality click traffic from their Internet-savvy users.

> **Google AdWords (http://adwords.google.com).** The Google AdWords program is a pioneer of performance-based paid search, and it can deliver both quantity and quality click traffic. It offers a variety of helpful tools, including customized reports, conversion tracking, geo-targeting, keyword suggestions, and ad diagnostics. An ad could cost as little as 1 cent per click, but you are more likely to pay at least 3 cents per click on most campaigns.

MSN adCenter (http://adcenter.msn.com). MSN's ad-Center program is a newer convert to the performance-based model, and although the volume of Internet searches performed on MSN does not currently approach Google's, the quality of traffic is very comparable. Also, MSN's adCenter program offers a variety of tools and options that include customized reports and geo-targeting, and it even allows advertisers certain demographic targeting options not currently available on many other search engines.

Yahoo! Search Marketing (www.overture.com). Yahoo! Search Marketing is one of the first and largest search and content networks on the Internet. Although the company has been around since 1994, Yahoo! didn't get aggressive about search marketing until 2002, when it began acquiring competing companies such as Inktomi and Overture. It stopped using Google's paid search service and began using its own technology in 2004; and, while it has only recently committed to adopting a performance-based paid search algorithm, Yahoo! certainly has the potential to match Google in terms of both quality and quantity.

Second-Tier Search and Content Networks

These search and content networks may not be as well-known or as popular as the first-tier engines, and the quality and volume of the traffic generated may not always be as high, but often-times these engines can deliver clicks at a lower cost, and in a business such as search marketing, that lower cost could translate to higher margins. These networks can be great for picking up some extra clicks at a good price, but I encourage you to be even more selective than you might normally be when selecting keywords and phrases (something discussed in more detail later). In particular, be very cautious using broad match on single keywords, as some of these algorithms seem to broad-match more widely than others, and this can sometimes result in less-relevant click traffic.

> **MIVA (www.miva.com).** This site has as its mission "Help Your Business Grow." It has several international sites, including separate locations in the United Kingdom, Germany, France, Spain, and other nations. MIVA offers a pay-per-click system as well as a pay-per-call system. If the companies you advertise (e.g., those in service industries, such as financial and investment companies or medical professionals) want to receive phone calls from prospective customers, consider MIVA.

> **Kanoodle (www.kanoodle.com).** Along with targeting ads based on geographic location of the prospective customers, the context of the ad, and keywords, Kanoodle offers one other innovative solution: targeting the behavior of prospective customers. The BehaviorTarget program identifies segments of Web surfers based on their online behavior, sending ads for specific products and services to individuals based on that behavior. For instance, if Kanoodle knows that someone has visited the site of a surfing shop in the past 30 days, it might deliver paid placement advertisements for surfboards and other equipment to that individual.

> **Enhance (www.enhance.com).** This network seeks to distinguish itself from the competition in two ways. First of all, the site claims that its click prices (with a minimum bid of 3 cents per click) are lower than those of most other networks. Second, it seeks to offer a higher level of

customer support than bigger competitors: Each customer gets a telephone number and access to an account representative who can help. Enhance has excellent customer service, and my experience has been that it can actually deliver a very high volume of clicks at a low price, but you must be very selective with the keywords you use, making certain that they are highly relevant.

Why choose one of the second-tier content networks? In some instances content networks like Kanoodle provide high-quality traffic for specialized subjects. For certain products or services, these networks might perform very well, so don't leave them out of your options.

I don't recommend that you start out, though, with second-tier search and content networks, because their volume and/or quality of traffic is sometimes much lower than that of their bigger competitors. It's safer to start out with the bigger players and then expand to one or more of these smaller sites after you secure a foothold in the market and have some experience managing search campaigns.

WHAT ARE MY SEARCH MARKETING OPTIONS?

Most search engines offer more than one way to place paid search ads on their networks. Text ads are the most common and the most effective, but some networks also allow you to place image ads, though I haven't had any success at all with them myself. When it comes to search marketing, a picture is definitely *not* worth a thousand words. Whatever type of ads you do run, however, you need to be aware of the venues for running them. The most common choices are search networks and content networks, so we should take a moment to describe them both.

Search Networks

We all know what a search engine is by now, but did you know that not all search pages are powered by their own search engine? Many search pages, and web sites with search functions, are powered not by their own search engines but by another search engine they partner up with to provide these search capabilities to their clients. CNN's web site, for instance, offers a search function powered by Yahoo! Those web sites that partner with a search engine to provide these services are part of that search engine's search network. When you run an ad on a search network, that ad could be displayed in the search results on hundreds of different search pages. Some search engines, like Google for instance, allow you to opt in or opt out of their search network (see Figure 3.5), which allows you to run your ad either on

Figure 3.5 Opting In or Out of Google's Search Network
Source: Screenshots © Google Inc. and are used with permission.

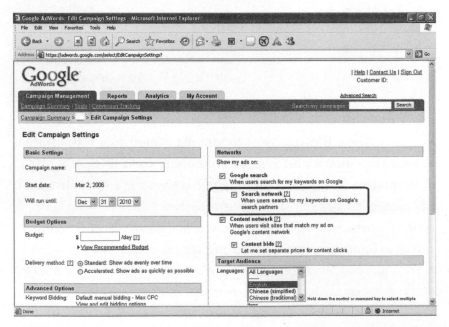

just the Google search pages or on all their partner search pages as well.

Content Networks

Content networks work a little differently from search engines. When you run your ad on a content network, it is not showing up in a list of search results in response to search terms matching the keywords or phrases you bid on. Instead, your ad is shown on web sites whose content matches the keywords you bid on. For example, if you are promoting an affiliate program for a jobs site and you bid on the keyword *resume*, your ad might appear on a web site dedicated to resume building. Some search engines (I'll use Google again as an example) will allow you to opt in or opt out of their content networks the same way you can opt in or out of their search networks, and they will even allow you to place separate bids for ads running on their content network (see Figure 3.6).

Google also offers you the flexibility of choosing exactly which content sites your ads appear on and has even offered, instead of the pay-per-click model, a *pay-per-impression program*, or CPM, in which advertisers pay a fixed cost for each 1,000 times an ad is shown on the Web page or pages where it appears.

Some content networks, including Google, give search marketers the option to advertise by CPM, but I generally advise against it. The CPM payment model is not tied to a measurable performance metric and is more commonly used to slowly build or maintain a level of brand recognition among a specific audience rather than to generate an immediate return on your investment. The pay-per-click bidding system allows you to control your costs and keep your spending levels below your expected returns. This is much more difficult to accomplish under a pay-per-impression system, and I recommend you avoid it.

Content networks can be a good source of additional traffic,

Figure 3.6 Opting In or Out of Google's Content Network and Separate Bids
Source: Screenshots © Google Inc. and are used with permission.

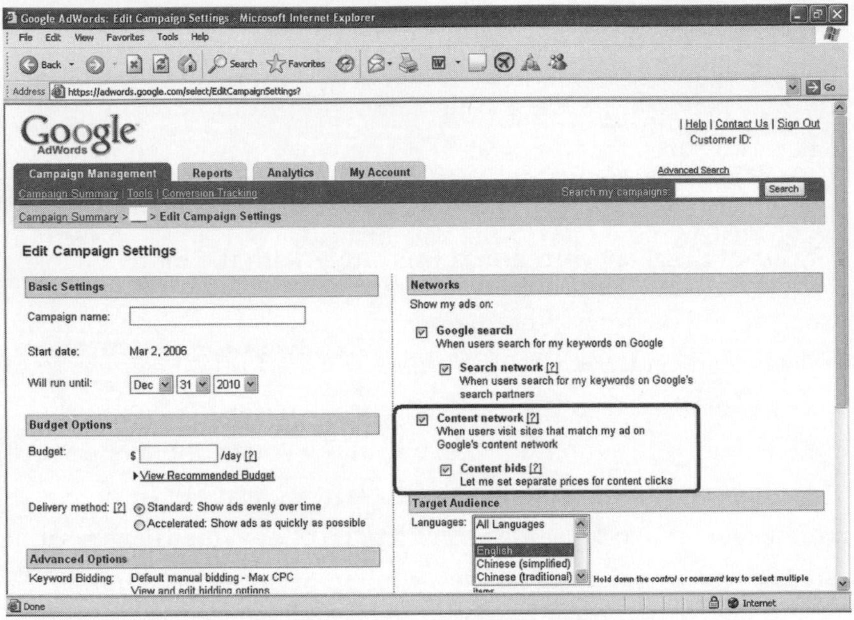

but not in all instances. In fact, I have had only one really successful content campaign in the few years I have been doing this. It earned nearly a thousand dollars a day for me while it lasted, so I encourage you to try these now and then, but be aware that it may be slightly more difficult to build profitable campaigns on the content networks than on the search networks.

WHY USE SEARCH MARKETING TO PROMOTE AFFILIATE PROGRAMS?

Search marketing works because it matches consumers' desires with a way to gratify them. When Web surfers look for something—say, an expensive pair of Italian shoes, they are presented with ads related to their search for, say, "Borelli shoes" that probably even contain the brand name of the shoes they're looking for in the main heading of the ad.

Learning the Lingo of PPC

In order to make money with PPC, it pays (literally) to know the language. Whenever you sign up for programs or read about them, you are presented with some basic terms that everyone seems to assume you know. I'm not going to make that assumption. I'm going to provide brief explanations of the most common terms along with the many alternative terms or phrases—it often seems each web site has its own way of speaking that's different from its competitors' lingo. Here are some of the basic terms you need to know:

- *Conversion ratio.* You might also see this referred to as *conversion rate.* The conversion rate refers to the number of individuals who click on an online ad and end up performing a specific action, such as making a purchase or filling out a registration form.
- *Click value.* I commonly call this the *margin* on a click. It's the difference between what you pay for a click and how much you make on that click. If you pay $1 per click for one campaign and 5 cents for another, it doesn't necessarily mean the 5-cent click is a better value. If you earn $1.75 per click with the $1 click and earn only 6 cents on the 5-cent click, the $1 click has a higher click value.
- *Cost per click.* The amount you actually pay for each click, as opposed to how much you bid per click.
- *Pay per click.* An advertising system in which advertisers pay for placing an ad based on the number of times someone clicks on it, as opposed to paying for each time the ad is viewed (per impression).

- *Return on investment (ROI).* Your return on your advertising investment (i.e., your earnings). If you spend $100 on a campaign and you get back $150, your ROI is 50 percent, or $50.

- *Landing page.* A landing page is the Web page that your link points to. It might be a link to a product description page on Amazon.com or Barnesandnoble.com or on some other merchant's web site.

- *Keywords.* Words or phrases that people enter when they search for something on a search engine. Also called *search terms*.

- *Negative keywords.* Words or phrases that will exclude searchers using those negative keywords from seeing your ads.

- *Performance tiers.* Tiers are levels of performance. If you deliver above a certain level of volume in a quarter, some advertisers will increase your commissions. Your commission slides depending on how well you do with them.

- *Natural search.* When you submit keywords to a web site and click the Search button, the results you get are a mixture of natural search and sponsored search (or paid search). The natural search results are the ones the search engine finds—not the ones people have paid for. Conversely, when you submit your web site to a search engine for free, it shows up on natural search results—if it is accepted.

- *Paid search* (also called *sponsored search*). These are ads that publishers like you and other advertisers have paid to have included alongside the natural search results.

- *Content-focused advertising*. Advertising that matches
to the content around them, which increases the chances
that the readers of the content will be interested in the con-
tent of the advertisement. Also called *contextual advertising*
or *content match advertising*.

These terms are intended as a starting point. You'll find a
wider selection of terms in this book's glossary.

Were it not for search marketing, you would be limited in the
number and types of affiliate programs you could join and earn
money on by the content of your web site. No sense trying to sell
fine Italian shoes on your astronomy web site. The ad space will
earn more money promoting relevant products, like telescopes,
than by trying to sell shoes. You could create lots of web sites,
each with unique and different content, but this requires quite an
investment in time and money.

With search marketing, you have access to an unlimited
variety of relevant audiences without the expense of creating or
popularizing your own variety of content sites. This flexibility
allows you to promote any product, any service, virtually any-
thing at all simply by bidding on a few (or in some cases a few
hundred) relevant keywords and displaying your ads automat-
ically to a relevant audience. Once your campaign is running
properly, it can continue to earn money with very little addi-
tional effort on your part, beyond simply monitoring the returns.
Some of my campaigns, once established, have earned tens of
thousands of dollars a month for months at a time with no
changes at all. Try getting a web site to perform like that without
constant attention.

In short, search marketing is faster, easier, and cheaper than setting up web sites on your own to advertise affiliate programs (although if you already own and operate a successful site, by all means use that site as well). In addition to these advantages, the potential of search marketing to generate income is limited only by your own intelligence, drive, and initiative.

In this chapter, you learned about many different types of paid search options. You were introduced to the major search and content networks, and you found out why search marketing should be such an integral part of your affiliate advertising business. Now we know about affiliate advertising, we know something about search marketing, and we know we want to use these two disciplines together to generate wealth. I guess it is finally time to get started.

In Chapter 4, I start to actually walk you through the process of joining affiliate networks; in Chapter 5, we begin comparing affiliate programs and choosing which of those programs you should join and promote first.

Part II

Launching
Your Advertising Campaign

Chapter 4

Joining Affiliate Networks

Now that you've been introduced to affiliate advertising and search marketing, it's time to take some concrete steps toward making it all happen. In this chapter, I walk you through the process of joining some affiliate networks, and because this is often the stage at which I receive the most phone calls from friends who try affiliate advertising, I am going to be as detailed as possible. Keep in mind, though, that web sites sometimes make changes to their application process. If you run into trouble, I have developed a Web resource to help ensure that up-to-date information and instructions are always available. That resource is the *Affiliate Millions* site at www.AffiliateMillions.com.

HOW TO JOIN AFFILIATE NETWORKS

There are dozens, if not hundreds, of affiliate networks available out there on the Internet for you to join. I can't provide you with step-by-step instructions on how to participate in each and every one of those networks, but I can walk you through the process with a few of my favorites. After joining a few of these sites with my help, you shouldn't have any problem taking yourself through

ss on your own with some of the many other networks
...ere.

Specifically, I am going to help you get started by walking
you through the process of joining four of my favorite networks: Commission Junction, Affiliate Fuel, Advertising.com, and
Amazon.com's Associates Central. Even though it isn't an affiliate network per se, Amazon.com runs one of the largest affiliate
programs on the Internet and offers a wide range of products.
Since Amazon runs this affiliate program on its own, not as part
of another affiliate network, I simply treat it as a network of one.

I should remind you here that the process of joining most of
these networks will go much smoother if you set up at least a simple web site of your own to represent your new business (a process described in Chapter 8). Most affiliate applications request
information about your web site, even when many of their affiliate programs will allow you to advertise their programs on
search engines without having a web site of your own. My own
web site, www.AffiliateMillions.com, has free web site templates
and can assist you in finding domain names and Web hosting sites.

After you join one or more of these networks—some may take
some time to approve you, so I recommend making good use of
the waiting time by joining at least a few—Chapter 5 revisits a
couple of these networks and teaches you how to search for and
select affiliate programs and to generate the tracking code you
will need in Chapter 6, when you start writing your ads.

Joining Commission Junction

Signing up with Commission Junction is not a complicated process, but if you are new to the industry you might have a hard
time determining exactly which program to join. The Commission

Junction home page divides its clients into two categories: advertisers and publishers. You might think at first—as I did—that you should sign up as an advertiser. After all, you will be advertising these affiliate programs, won't you? As far as Commission Junction is concerned, though, the term *advertiser* applies solely to those companies that sign up with Commission Junction to launch affiliate advertising programs for their own web sites. The businesses and individuals who apply to Commission Junction in order to promote these affiliate programs on search engines or on their own web sites, yourself included, are *publishers*. Think of the term *publisher* as a synonym for *affiliate*, and remember that you will be publishing these ads, either on your own site or on the search and content networks we join in Chapter 6.

In any case, to become a publisher with Commission Junction, you need to fill out its application form. You can get to the form in one of two ways. The first way is to burrow into the site using the following three steps:

1. Go to the home page (www.cj.com) and click the "Publishers link" on the lower center of your screen (see Figure 4.1).
2. When the Publishers page appears, click on "Learn more about CJ Marketplace" (see Figure 4.2).
3. When the CJ Marketplace page appears, click on "Click here" in the paragraph on publishers (see Figure 4.3) and you will be taken to the application form page.

The second option is to jump directly to the application page. You can point your browser directly to the application page you want at https://signup.cj.com/member/publisherSignUp.do.

The only advantage of not going directly to the sign-up page

Figure 4.1 Click on the "e-Publishers" Link
Source: Commission Junction, CJ.com

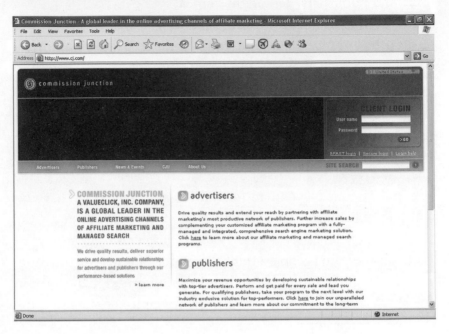

is that you can read some background on CJ Marketplace, which is the program you'll be applying to join. In either case, whether you go directly to the application page or not, once you are there you will need to fill out the two-part application.

Step 1: Publisher Application. Step 1 of the application (shown in Figure 4.4) is a simple form requesting your language preference, country, and functional currency. When you are finished, click "Next."

Step 2: Verifications. After you click "Next," you will be taken to the second page, "Publisher Application: Step 2 of 2." This is somewhat lengthy, but you'll have it filled out in no time.

Figure 4.2 Click on "Learn More about the CJ Marketplace"
Source: Commission Junction, CJ.com

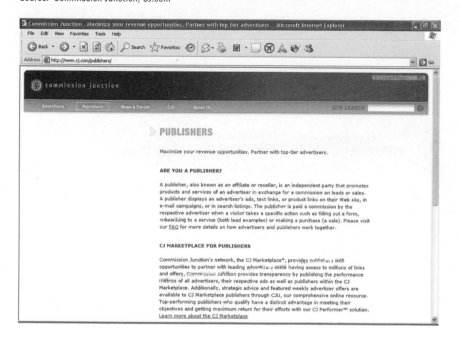

The top of page 2 consists of three check boxes to verify you have read and accepted Commission Junction's Publisher Service Agreement (PSA) and privacy policy and that you are at least 18 years of age (see Figure 4.5). First and foremost, be sure to read and accept the PSA. You will need to read the PSA all the way to the bottom, where the Accept button appears, and click on it. Then you will need to read and accept the Privacy Policy, making sure to check the box indicating you have done so when you are finished. Finally, you will need to verify that you are at least 18 years of age (assuming you are) by checking the appropriate box.

Site Information. Below the verifications comes the next section of the form, the Site Information section. If you do in fact have a web

Figure 4.3 Click on the "Click here" Link in the Paragraph on Publishers
Source: Commission Junction, CJ.com

ABOUT US ≫ CJ MARKETPLACE

Commission Junction's network, the CJ Marketplace, provides high rewards for publishers and extensive reach for advertisers while remaining the industry's most productive and only truly global network. Supported by our commitment to network quality, the CJ Marketplace provides an environment that fosters excellence in business practices while safeguarding the brands of our clients.

Commission Junction provides transparency by publishing the performance metrics of all advertisers, publishers and ads within the CJ Marketplace. This approach provides advertisers and publishers a way to gauge the value of their existing and potential relationships by using two key metrics – average earnings per 100 clicks (EPC) and network earnings.

By joining the CJ Marketplace, publishers and advertisers have a sophisticated, Web-based interface to access information, analyze results and manage their programs for success in real time. Read our FAQ for more details the CJ Marketplace.

ADVERTISERS
Create your program description with a compelling call to action, define your program terms, review publisher applications, and analyze your program's performance using our comprehensive reporting tools. Also tap into our comprehensive online resource, CJU Online, to learn about program strategies, connect with publishes and catch up on the latest industry news. Click here to find out more about how you can become a Commission Junction advertiser.

PUBLISHERS
Apply to join advertisers' programs, get immediate access to their entire inventory of links and begin placing their offers on your Web sites, in e-mail campaigns, or in search listings. In addition, strategic advice and featured weekly advertiser offers are available through CJU Online, our comprehensive online resource. Click here to join our unparalleled network of publishers and learn more about our commitment to the long-term success of top-performing publishers.

site, you may list it here. If you do not have a web site and intend to use search marketing to directly promote the affiliate programs you join, then this form is not really designed to accept your application, as the web site name and URL fields are required, but you can try a method I have successfully used to join some affiliate networks in the past.

Try entering "Search Engine Marketer" in the name field and the URL of a search engine in the required URL field, and then make it clear in the web site description field that you do not own

Figure 4.4   Step 1 of Commission Junction's Publisher Application
Source: Commission Junction, CJ.com

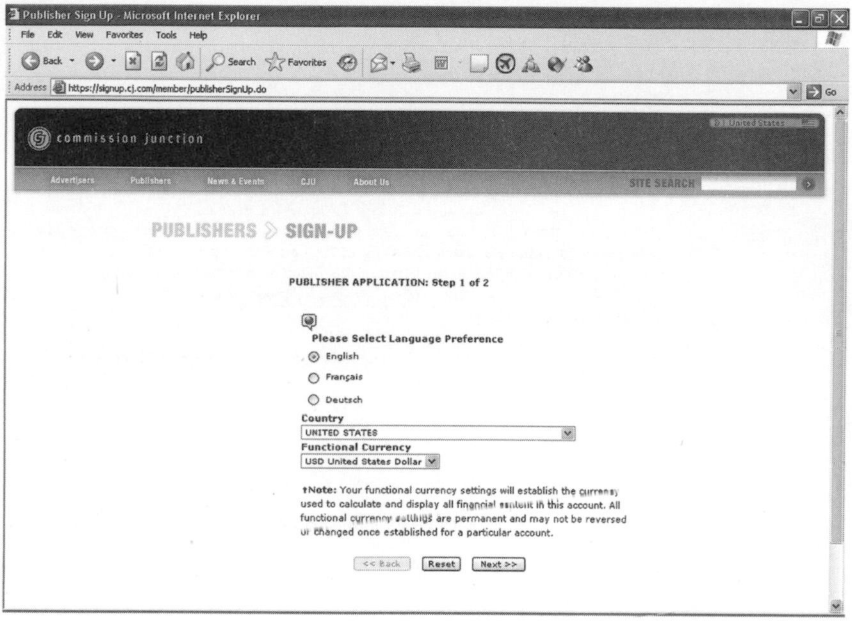

a web site of your own, but that you will be purchasing ad space on search engines and content networks. This method will allow you to submit the application for consideration even though you do not own a web site.

Some networks will approve you; others may choose not to. If an affiliate network that you really want to join turns you down just because you do not have a web site, you may want to consider starting one. On my own site, www.AffiliateMillions.com, I offer free web site templates and assistance in finding domain names and web site hosting.

In the Category field (see Figure 4.6), select Web Services > Search Engine. Then be sure to check Search Engine Marketing, along with any other promotional methods you might use, in the "Define your promotional methods" portion of the Site

Figure 4.5 Verifications
Source: Commission Junction, CJ.com

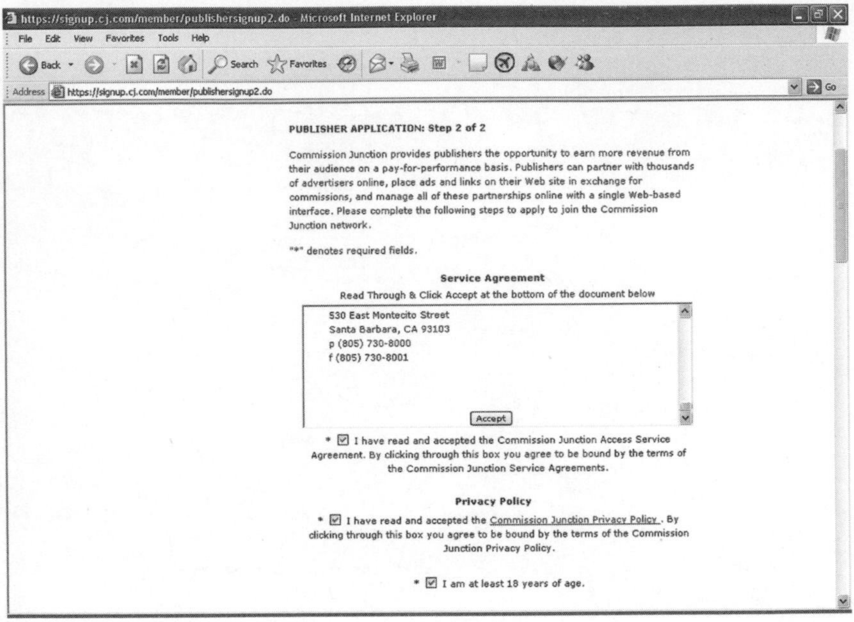

Information section. Simply answer no to the question about site incentives unless you have or are developing a site that will offer any kind of incentives.

Contact Information. Simply enter your name and address.

Company Information. Unless you have a separate business entity to enter, you may enter your personal information here, including using your own name for the Organization Name field. When you come to the Tax ID field, you may enter your social security number unless, once again, you have a separate business identity complete with its own federal tax identification number. Then be sure to select Individual/Sole Proprietor from the drop-down menu for Tax Classification (see Figure 4.7).

Figure 4.6 Site Information
Source: Commission Junction, CJ.com

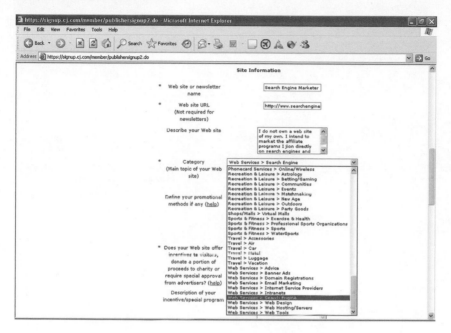

Payment Information. Finally, in the Payment Information section you will need to select your preferred payment type from the drop-down box (see Figure 4.8). You may choose whatever form of payment you like, but be aware that only direct deposit is completely free of charge. Depending on which method of payment you choose, you will need to fill in the relevant details. You are now ready to submit your application.

When you are finished filling out the form, click on "Accept Terms." The Publisher Application Submitted page appears. As the first paragraph of this page explains, Commission Junction will send an e-mail (to the address you provided) containing your account number, your user name (the same as the e-mail address you already supplied), and your password. When this e-mail arrives, you can log on to your CJ Account Manager™ and start

Figure 4.7 Company Information
Source: Commission Junction, CJ.com

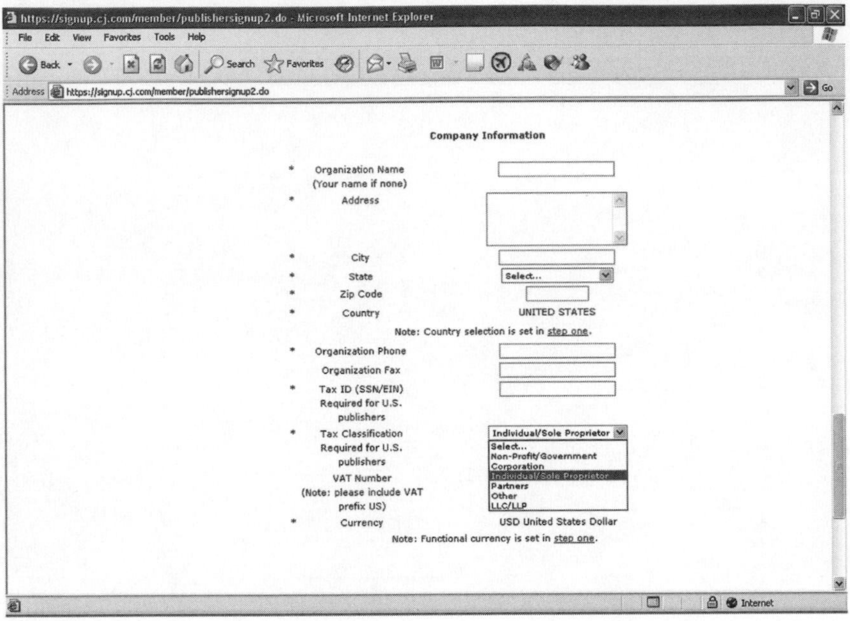

looking for affiliate programs to join. Instead of waiting around for that e-mail to arrive, though, let's continue on and join a few more affiliate networks.

NOTE: You may have noticed while you were on the Commission Junction home page that there was a link for something called the BFAST login. Bfast was originally a ValueClick company called Be Free, which was in operation before ValueClick acquired Commission Junction. Today, Commission Junction is definitely the big player, and I rarely use Bfast. I find its user interface less intuitive than Commission Junction's, and the selection is much broader on Commission Junction as well. There is one affiliate program at Bfast that I had good luck with early on in my career, though, and you may find it worth the effort of

Figure 4.8   Payment Information
Source: Commission Junction, CJ.com

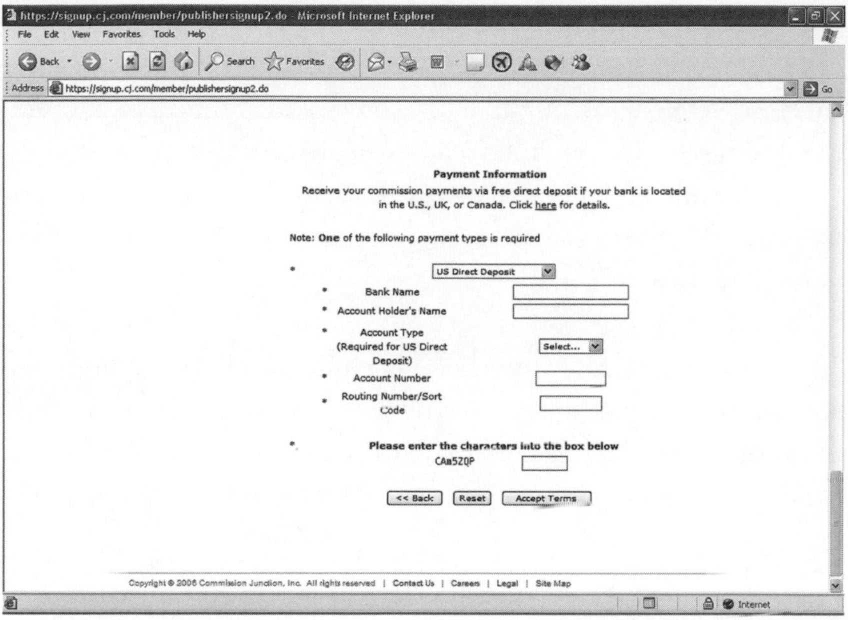

joining just to participate. Barnes & Noble is the affiliate program of which I speak, and I do recommend it to beginners, as it has reasonable commissions, a wide variety of products to market, and achievable performance tiers.

Joining AffiliateFuel.com

Affiliate Fuel is a premium affiliate network that accepts only high-quality web sites with established traffic, so if you are looking to submit a site of your own, it had better be top-notch or you are just wasting your time. If you are looking to join just as a search marketer, Affiliate Fuel is one of those networks that considered my application to promote its affiliate programs using only search marketing. It has very strict rules, however, about which programs can and cannot be marketed in this way, as well as a long list of protected keywords you cannot bid on. Break these rules and you will be thrown out of the network very quickly, and likely you will not be paid for your fraudulent traffic. Obey the rules, however, and you can enjoy some of the highest payouts on the Internet for the qualified leads you are able to generate.

To become a publisher with Affiliate Fuel, you will need to visit its application page at www.affiliatefuel.com/cgi-bin/newhost (see Figure 4.9).

Login Information. The application itself does not appear until you scroll down the page, to just below the Apply Today! icon. It starts with the Login Information section, where you simply need to choose your user name and password before moving along to the

Figure 4.9 Affiliate Fuel's Application Page
Source: © 2001–2006 Affiliate Fuel Corp, www.AffiliateFuel.com

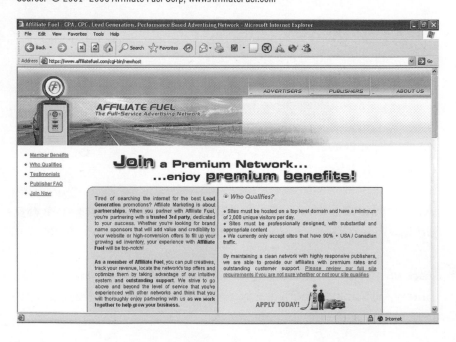

Figure 4.10 Fill in the Login Information and Account
Information Sections of the Application
Source: © 2001–2006 Affiliate Fuel Corp, www.AffiliateFuel.com

Account Information section. Both these sections appear in Figure 4.10.

Account Information. This section is fairly straightforward as well. Enter your name, social security or tax ID number, and address and contact information. Be sure to fill in your company name if you have one, and specify to whom Affiliate Fuel should make out the checks. Even if you have a business name, you may want to use your personal name here, unless you have a business account at a bank or credit union that will accept checks written out to your business. Finally, choose the minimum amount your account will earn before Affiliate Fuel sends you a check (you will not receive more than one check a month, at most, but the company will hold off sending your monthly check if your account balance has not yet reached the minimum check amount).

Website Information. Enter the name and URL of your web site; if you do not have a web site of your own, this section will require the same method we discussed earlier. Namely, you will enter the Website URLs of the search and content networks on which you intend to run these ads, identify yourself as a search marketer in the Website Name field, select Search Engine from the Website Category drop-down menu and identify your search marketing strategy in the Describe Your Site field (see Figure 4.11). If you do not have a prior search marketing record from which to draw some statistics to show your proficiency, you may need to leave the last two fields in this section blank. If you are turned down as a result, do not despair. You can return and reapply at a later date, when you have some statistics about the number of impressions your ads typically receive per day, and what level of traffic you generate from these impressions.

Opt-In Email. Unless you do in fact have a newsletter or an e-mail list, you may simply leave this entire section blank.

How Can We Help? This section asks only that you identify the types of offers you are looking for (see Figure 4.12).

Figure 4.11 Website Information and Opt-In Email Sections of the Application
Source: © 2001–2006 Affiliate Fuel Corp, www.AffiliateFuel.com

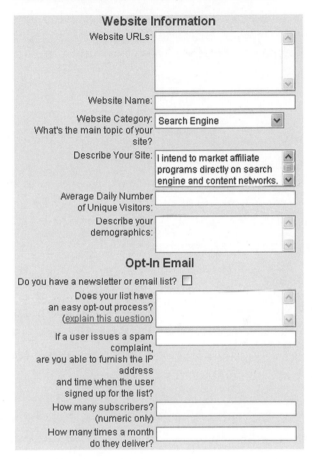

Sign Up. All that remains now is to read and accept the Terms and Conditions, enter the verification code shown (see example in Figure 4.12), and click on the Sign Up button at the bottom of the application. Please note, however, that you will also need to submit a W9 form, and instructions for doing so appear just below the Sign Up button.

Figure 4.12   How Can We Help and Verification Sections of the Application
Source: © 2001–2006 Affiliate Fuel Corp, www.AffiliateFuel.com

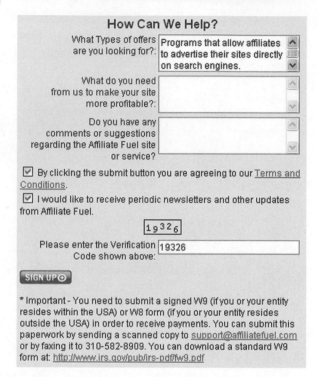

While you wait to see whether you are accepted into Affiliate Fuel's network, you may continue on to another affiliate network: Advertising.com.

Joining Advertising.com

Advertising.com is another one of my favorite affiliate networks. I recommend it because I personally have been very successful with this company, particularly early in my career, when some of my campaigns with Advertising.com affiliate programs provided me with my first big successes. The programs tend to pay well and have high conversion rates, so don't miss out on the opportunities presented to you.

To join Advertising.com's affiliate network, you will need to visit its publishers page at https://publisher.advertising.com and click on the Join Now! button on the left-hand side of the screen, just beneath the Sign In section. This will take you to the application page, where you will first complete the Account Information section.

Account Information. By now you are familiar with this type of form (see Figure 4.13). Simply choose a user name and a password and fill in your contact and payout information as before.

Channel Selection. The next portion of the application is the Channel Selection section. Here you will simply check the Affiliate box (see Figure 4.14) and click on Continue.

Affiliate Site Information. The next page is the Affiliate Site Information page (see Figure 4.15). Fill in your web site information in the fields requested, or use the methods discussed previously to indicate that you market affiliate programs directly through other search and content networks. The Monthly Impressions field is required, so if you do not have your own web site, you will need to estimate the number of ad views you can deliver through search marketing. When you are finished, click Continue.

Verify Application. The last page that now appears is the Verify Application page. Simply double-check all the information entered. Then read and accept the Terms and Conditions and click continue to submit your application.

Figure 4.13 Account Information Section of the Advertising.com Publisher Application
Source: Advertising.com

Account Information

Choose a Username:	[_____] *
Choose a Password:	[_____] *
Confirm Password:	[_____] *

Company Name:	[_____] *	**Payout Information**	
Primary URL:	[_____] *	Contact First Name:	[_____] *
Phone:	[_____] *	Contact Last Name:	[_____] *
Fax:	[_____]	Street Address:	[_____] *
Email:	[_____] *		[_____]
Secondary Email Addresses:	[_____]	City:	[_____] *
		State/Province:	[Please Choose] ▾ *
Intended Audience:	[Please Choose] ▾ *	Other State/Province:	[_____]
		Postal Code:	[_____] *
		Country:	[Please Choose] ▾ *
		Payee Name:	[_____] *
		(What is this?) Tax ID:	[_____]
		Minimum Check:	25.00 ▾

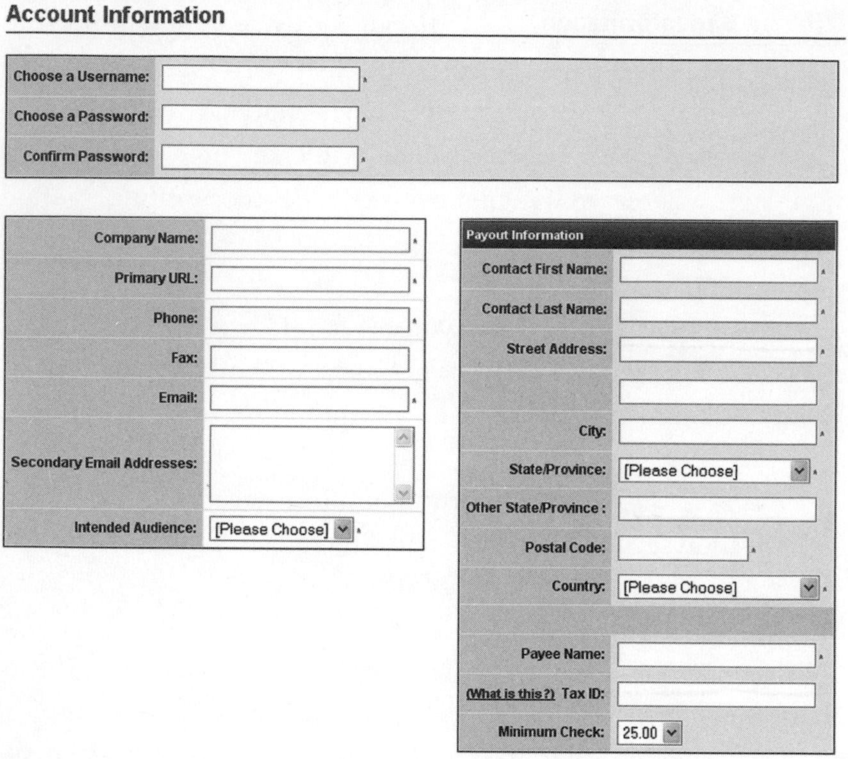

Figure 4.14 Channel Selection Section of the Advertising.com Publisher Application
Source: Advertising.com

Channel Selection

☑ **Affiliate** - Centrally hosted solution includes strategic campaign analysis and reporting tools to help you ensure your greatest earnings.

☐ **Web** - Automatic inventory fulfillment helps ensure your inventory never goes unsold.

☐ **Email** - A unique and diverse selection of quality advertisements for inclusion in your permission-based publications.

☐ **Search** - Partnerships with top advertisers and agencies drive incremental advertising revenue for search engines.

[Reset]   [Continue]

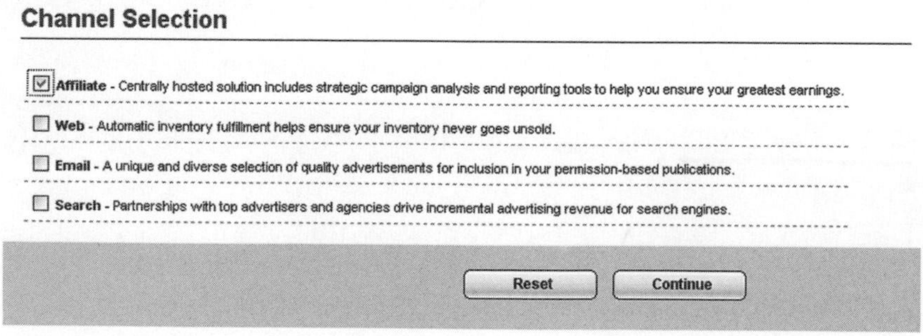

Figure 4.15 Affiliate Site Information Page of the Advertising.com Publisher Application
Source: Advertising.com

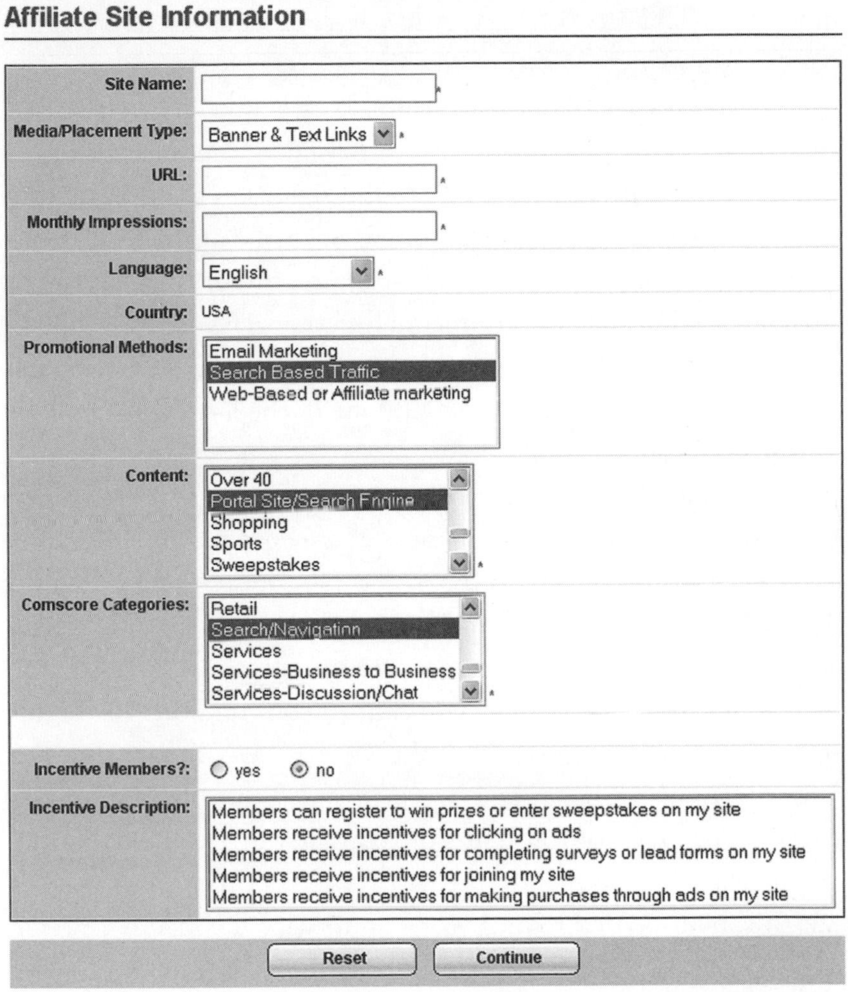

Affiliate Site Information

Site Name:	[ ] ^
Media/Placement Type:	Banner & Text Links ⌄ ^
URL:	[ ] ^
Monthly Impressions:	[ ] ^
Language:	English ⌄ ^
Country:	USA
Promotional Methods:	Email Marketing Search Based Traffic Web-Based or Affiliate marketing
Content:	Over 40 Portal Site/Search Engine Shopping Sports Sweepstakes ^
Comscore Categories:	Retail Search/Navigation Services Services-Business to Business Services-Discussion/Chat ^
Incentive Members?:	○ yes ⦿ no
Incentive Description:	Members can register to win prizes or enter sweepstakes on my site Members receive incentives for clicking on ads Members receive incentives for completing surveys or lead forms on my site Members receive incentives for joining my site Members receive incentives for making purchases through ads on my site

| Reset | Continue |

nat you have finished applying to Advertising.com, I
ist program I'd like to encourage you to join before we
Chapter 5. This is Amazon.com's program.

Joining Amazon.com's Associates Central Program

As I stated earlier, Amazon.com's Associates Central is not technically an affiliate network. I'm listing Associates Central in this
chapter because even though it offers only one affiliate program,
it does more business than most affiliate networks can generate
with all their affiliate programs put together. The company is big,
has a wide product base, and operates one of the most marketable
affiliate programs on the Web, with one of the largest selection of
products.

Associates Central also offers two choices of commission
structure: Classic and Performance. These commission structures
are adjusted from time to time, so you should compare them at
the end of each quarter before deciding which to join, but generally speaking, the Performance structure, which includes performance incentives that bring you higher commissions for higher
sales volume, is preferable to the Classic, which is a flat-rate
option.

The Amazon.com affiliate program is an excellent one for
beginners to join because of the wide range of products to market,
which can all be tied to and working toward a collective performance tier structure. In other words, all your various campaigns
for Amazon can help the other Amazon campaigns by helping
you reach a higher performance tier and raise the payouts across
the board.

Also, Amazon's Associates Central not only welcomes affiliates who do search engine marketing, but when you log on to
the site (http://affiliate-program.amazon.com) and click Perfor-

mance Tips in the list of links on the left-hand side of th
you find an entire section of tips for search engine mar
You can read case studies of businesses that have become Ama-
zon.com affiliates and boosted their business by promoting Ama-
zon.com merchandise. There's also a set of discussion boards
where associates help one another with tips and advice.

To join Amazon's Associates Central, you will need to visit the
Join Associates page, by either going directly to http://affiliate-
program.amazon.com/gp/associates/join or, more simply, clicking on the Join Associates link at the bottom of Amazon.com's
home page. Once there, you will want to click on "Want to Join?
Click here for easy registration" (see Figure 4.16).

Figure 4.16   Join Associates Page
Source: Amazon.com

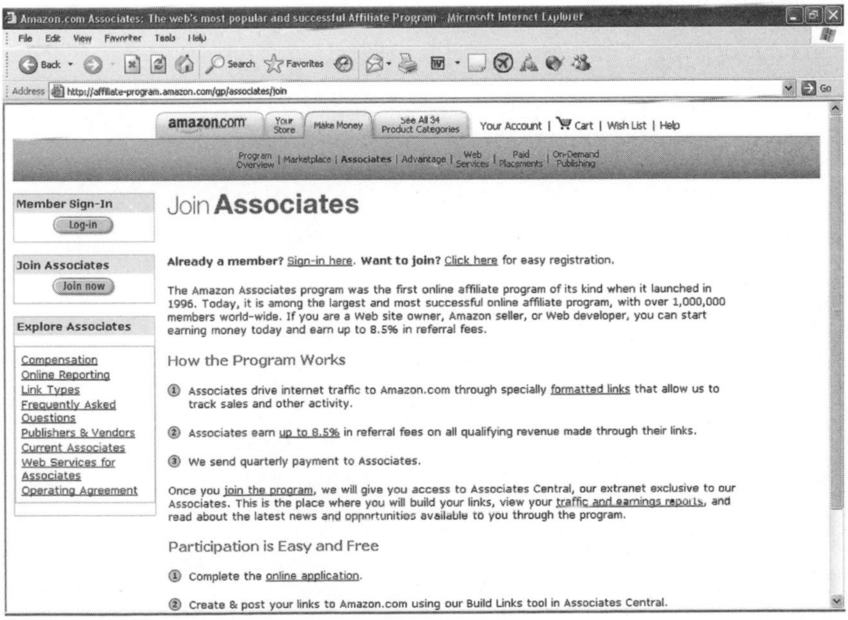

Account Info/Sign In. Once you have clicked on "Want to Join? Click here for easy registration," you will be taken to the Associates Central sign-in page. If you already have an account with Amazon under the e-mail address you would like to use, you may sign into Associates Central using that e-mail address and password. If not, you may enter your e-mail address, and you will then be taken to a quick and simple registration page before you are able to sign in.

Your Contact Information. After you have successfully signed in, you will be taken to the general information page of the application, the first section of which is Your Contact Information, a straightforward request for your name and contact information (see Figure 4.17). When you are finished, scroll down to the Your Web Site Profile portion of the application.

Figure 4.17   Your Contact Information Portion of the Application
Source: Amazon.com

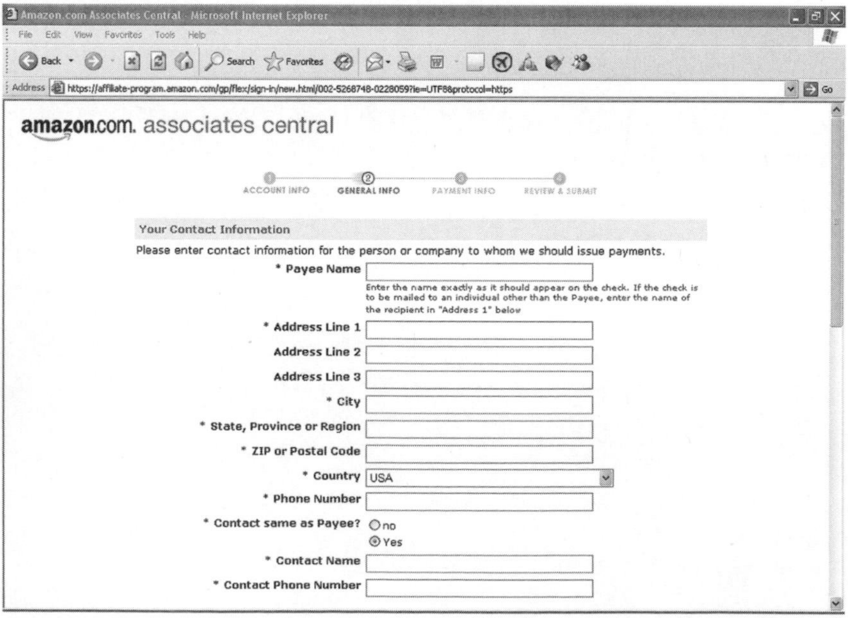

Your Web Site Profile. Here you will enter the information about your web site if you have one, or you will fill out the form indicating the search engines on which you intend to place paid search ads (see Figure 4.18). Amazon is a search marketing–friendly affiliate program, so this shouldn't present any real problems for you. When you are finished filling out this portion of the form, click Continue.

Your Payee Tax Information. After clicking Continue on the screen titled Your Web Site Profile, you will arrive at the payment information page, the first section of which is Your Payee Tax Information (see Figure 4.19). Simply enter your name or business name in the Tax Name field, type your social security or tax ID number in the Tax ID Number field, and make the appropriate

Figure 4.18   Your Web Site Profile Portion of the Application
Source: Amazon.com

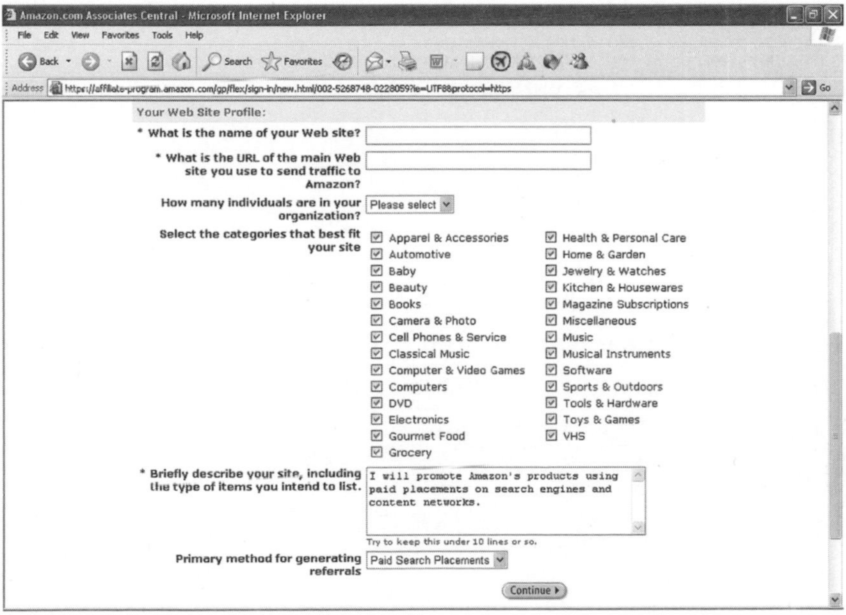

Figure 4.19 Your Payee Tax Information Portion of the Application
Source: Amazon.com

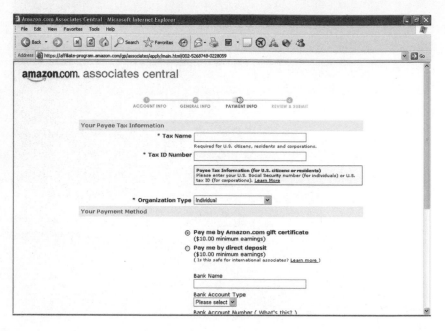

selection from the Organization Type drop-down menu (you'll probably choose Individual). Once you're finished, scroll down to Your Payment Method.

Your Payment Method. Finally, under Your Payment Method, you may select from three different payment options (see Figure 4.20). Direct deposit has a clear advantage over the pay-by-check option, which incurs a service fee, so if you have a bank account and are comfortable with the technology, then this is the option I recommend. Once you are finished, click Continue to submit your application.

Review and Submit. Before Amazon accepts your application, it will display all of the information previously entered. Review this information carefully, then read and accept the Associates

Figure 4.20   Your Payment Method Portion of the Application
Source: Amazon.com

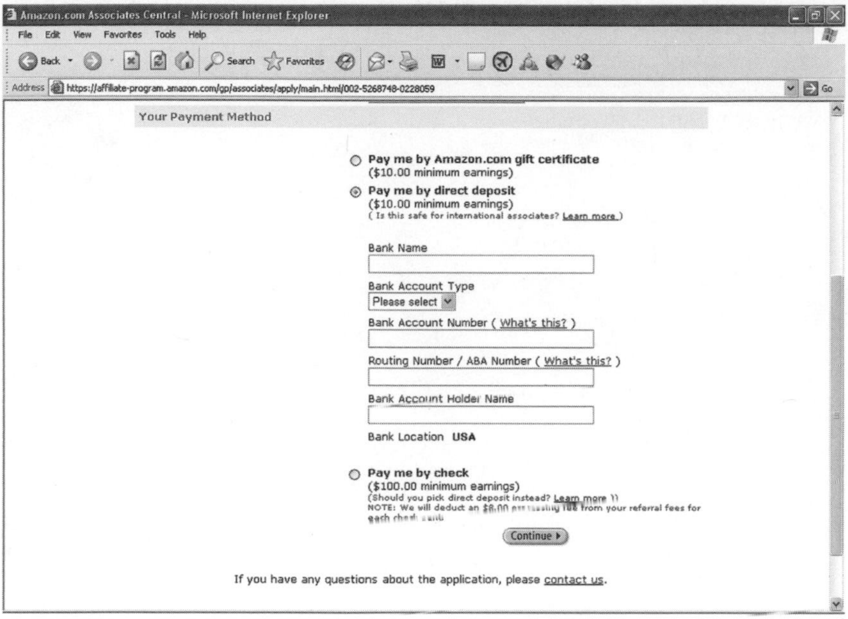

Operating Agreement beneath your information, and click on Continue to re-submit your reviewed application for consideration.

Other Affiliate Networks

There are, of course, other affiliate networks that might work well for you, and I provide a comprehensive and up-to-date list of affiliate networks on the *Affiliate Millions* web site at www .affiliatemillions.com. For now, though, I think you are off to a good start.

Hopefully by now, one or more of the affiliate networks you have just submitted information to has accepted your application and you are ready to begin searching for individual affiliate programs to join. In Chapter 5, I walk you through the process of selecting affiliate programs for some of the networks to which you've just applied.

Chapter 5

Joining Affiliate Programs

In preceding chapters you have learned about affiliate advertising and search marketing, and you have even begun joining some affiliate networks. Now it's time to go a step further and learn how to search for, choose, and join individual affiliate programs. I'll take you through the whole process with a couple of the affiliate networks we joined in Chapter 4, as the process varies a bit from network to network.

Before you get started joining these programs, I want to talk a little about what you should look for in, and what you should know about, different affiliate programs.

WHAT TO LOOK FOR IN AN AFFILIATE PROGRAM

When you are looking for an affiliate program to market, you're better off starting with a product you know about and are familiar with. When the time comes to start writing your ads, personal knowledge of the product or service you are marketing is a big advantage.

wledgeable about the Product or Service

As you search for potential affiliate programs to join and market, keep in mind that the more you know about the products or services offered, the better. This is especially important when you are new to the business. The more you know about the product— what people like or dislike about it, how it compares to competing products in price, performance, and value, and what sets it apart from the competition—the easier it will be for you to write effective ad copy and identify the appropriate keywords and phrases to trigger these ads. As you become more familiar with this process, you may eventually be able to rely on your own research to educate yourself on potential new affiliate programs, but in the beginning, when you have so much else to learn, it will pay to focus on products and services you already know quite well.

Be Knowledgeable about the Affiliate Program

Make sure you have a clear understanding of all aspects of the affiliate programs you advertise before you start running ads. Commission structures, payment methods, and a host of other concerns should be addressed before you actually start paying to promote any affiliate program.

Commission Structure. The most important of these concerns is, of course, the commission structure itself. Make sure you know what your goal is. More specifically, make sure you know what the affiliate program will pay you for, and how much. Will you receive a percentage of sales or just a percentage of revenue? (Revenue is the net profit on the sale, not the entire sale price.) Are you paid for downloads, form completions? Are your commissions tied to paid memberships or free registrations? Speaking of registrations, will you be paid for each registration or only for those that go on to become active members? Does the program have performance tiers or bonuses, and, if so, what must you do to trigger them?

Payment Terms and Methods. The standard in the industry is for advertisers or affiliate networks to issue payments every 30 days. If you see terms that specify 60 or 90 days, you should be aware that you will be spending on advertisements for up to three months before you ever see a dime in return, and you need to plan accordingly. Do the companies with whom you do business charge for payment by check? Do they offer direct deposit? As a general rule, search marketers, including myself, prefer to receive payments in the form of electronic fund transfers that go directly into their checking accounts. Most advertisers and networks will allow this, as well as the option of receiving a check in the mail, but they generally charge extra for mailing a paper check.

Minimum Balance for Payment. Almost all advertisers issue payments only when the affiliate has reached a minimum level (often $25). Many offer lower limits for direct deposit than they do for checks.

Provisions for Rollovers and Carryovers. Rollovers and carryovers occur when an affiliate doesn't meet the minimum balance required to receive a payment.

Payment for Returning Referrals (Referral Period). Sometimes, you'll refer customers to a site who won't buy anything right away. They'll look around other sites and make a purchase on a future visit. Look for programs in which merchants have a referral period during which they will issue you a commission if one of the people you have referred makes a purchase on a future return visit.

Chargebacks and Returns. Chargebacks and returns are the bane of all retailers, but they are a fact of life. The person who buys something as a result of a referral by you might well return it eventually. Most merchants have a *chargeback period*—a period of time in which the customer can return the product for a refund. If so, your commission will be debited. Merchants who have a return policy tend to have a better conversion rate, because consumers are more likely to buy from them. But the same policy might result in your commission being taken away if the item is returned. There's nothing you can do about such a policy, but it's good to be aware of it so you aren't surprised when a percentage of your commissions are eventually reversed.

Quality of a Company's Online Presentation. Would you buy a product from the company you advertise as an affiliate? You should refer to merchants that have an effective online presentation—lots of photos, clear information about brand names, model numbers, sizes, colors, and other variations, and a clear purchase path. The *purchase path* is the path that leads from the product description page to the checkout area. Don't send customers to a site that is loaded down with lots of intrusive pop-up ads and other distractions. These distractions will lower your conversion rate. Also, know whether your affiliate program offers special discounts and promotions. Besides inducing purchases, you can mention those incentives in your own affiliate ad.

Quality of the Merchandise. Affiliate advertising is an impersonal thing. It's not like going into a retail store and testing the merchandise to see how it feels and looks. It's actually easy to lose sight of the fact that you are promoting real products and services. But quality is something to keep in mind when you are choosing products to promote. Just imagine how you would feel if you were referred by a web site to a product that turned out to be of inferior quality? Poor quality or overpriced merchandise is more likely to be returned. Check for testimonials and references from existing customers to find out about the quality of goods.

Reputation. Obviously, you don't want to strike up a relationship with a merchant that isn't going to pay you on time or one that has generated a slew of complaints from other customers and affiliates. If you sign up with an affiliate program through a network, chances are you won't run into many bad apples. Nevertheless, you should try to avoid merchants who already have a bad reputation. If you can find other affiliates (through a discussion board or newsgroup) who use the merchant, ask about that company's reputation.

IDENTIFYING AND JOINING THE RIGHT AFFILIATE PROGRAMS

Okay, let's get started. You've learned some best practices for vetting the affiliate programs before promoting them; now it's time to roll up our sleeves and actually start looking for some programs to sign up with. As promised, I'll walk you through the process with some of the affiliate networks you joined in Chapter 4.

Commission Junction

Commission Junction is a great network to start off with, as it offers hundreds of affiliate programs, an intuitive interface, and a variety of methods that you can use to compare programs against each other. After logging into the CJ Account Manager, with the e-mail address and password you provided during the registration process, you'll be taken to the CJ Marketplace home page (see Figure 5.1).

Figure 5.1 CJ Marketplace's Home Page
Source: Commission Junction

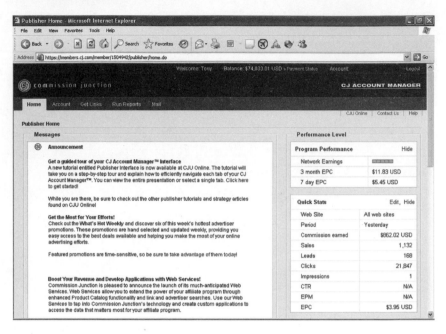

This page can provide you with a lot of useful and customizable statistics once you are in business for a while, but for now you'll notice it doesn't have much to offer. Let's just move straight ahead to the affiliate programs by clicking on the Get Links tab beneath the Commission Junction logo. This should bring you to the General Categories page (Figure 5.2), where you will see Commission Junction's affiliate programs broken out into different categories and subcategories.

There are lots of different categories to explore, and based on some of the advice I've given you earlier in this chapter you should be ready to explore this list. Since I don't know which of these categories might hold the most interest for you, I will select one with broad appeal for the purposes of moving forward with my example. I recommend clicking on the Commerce category in

Figure 5.2   Commission Junction's General Categories Page
Source: Commission Junction

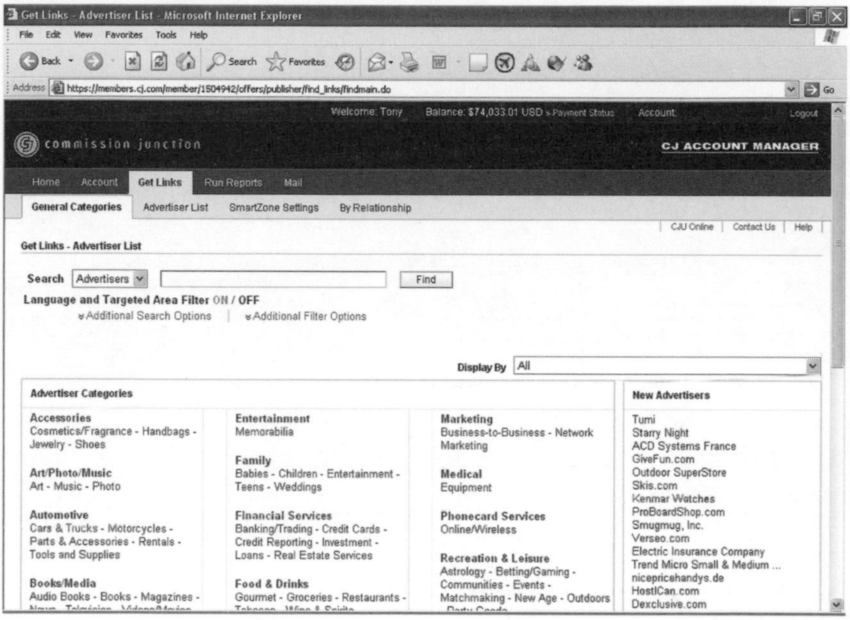

the first column to begin. This should take you to an Advertiser Search Results page (see Figure 5.3).

This page lists all the affiliate programs Commission Junction has categorized as commerce sites. The first thing you might notice is that each of these programs can be measured against the others by three different performance metrics. These performance metrics are "3 Month EPC," "7 Day EPC," and "Network Earnings." At first glance, the *earnings per hundred clicks* (EPC) metrics might look the most finely grained and therefore the most useful, but as a search marketer with no way of knowing how much these clicks cost to generate, this metric is not particularly helpful in selecting programs. A more useful metric for selecting programs is *network earnings*. A sliding scale of one to five bars (look under the Network Earnings column in Figure 5.3), with five

Figure 5.3 Commission Junction's Advertiser Search Results Page
Source: Commission Junction

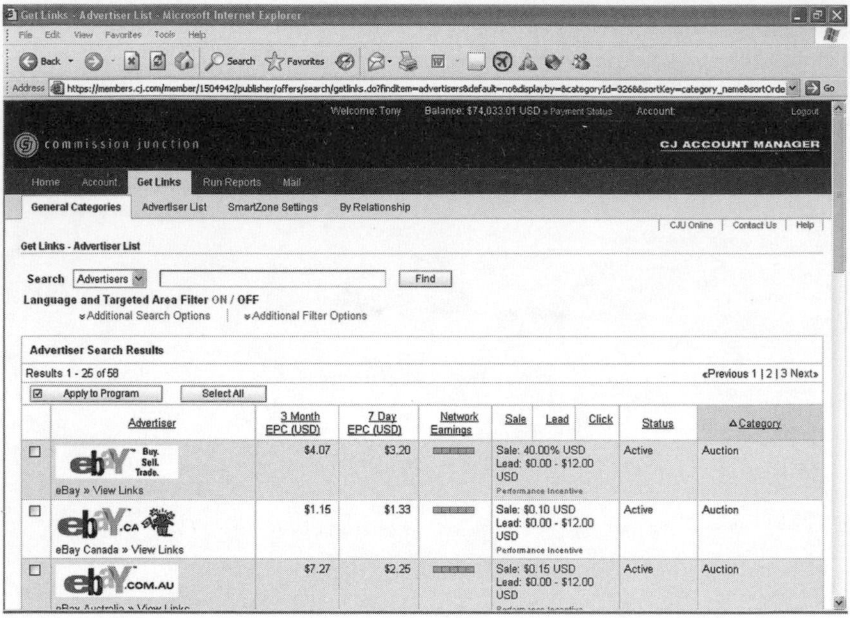

being the highest, indicates which programs are generating the most earnings. The bigger the pie, after all, the easier it is to cut yourself a slice.

Notice that the top honors in the Network Earnings column in Figure 5.3 go to a superb affiliate program with a five-bar rating: eBay! This is an excellent program to join, as it offers an unlimited variety of products to promote, has a competitive commission structure, and holds unparalleled name recognition. Let's investigate this program further, proceeding as though I were not recommending it.

By clicking on the advertiser's name or image in the Advertiser column on the results page, you can open the Advertiser Detail page shown in Figure 5.4.

Be sure to read all the details of the affiliate program, especially

Figure 5.4 Advertiser Detail Page for eBay
Source: Commission Junction

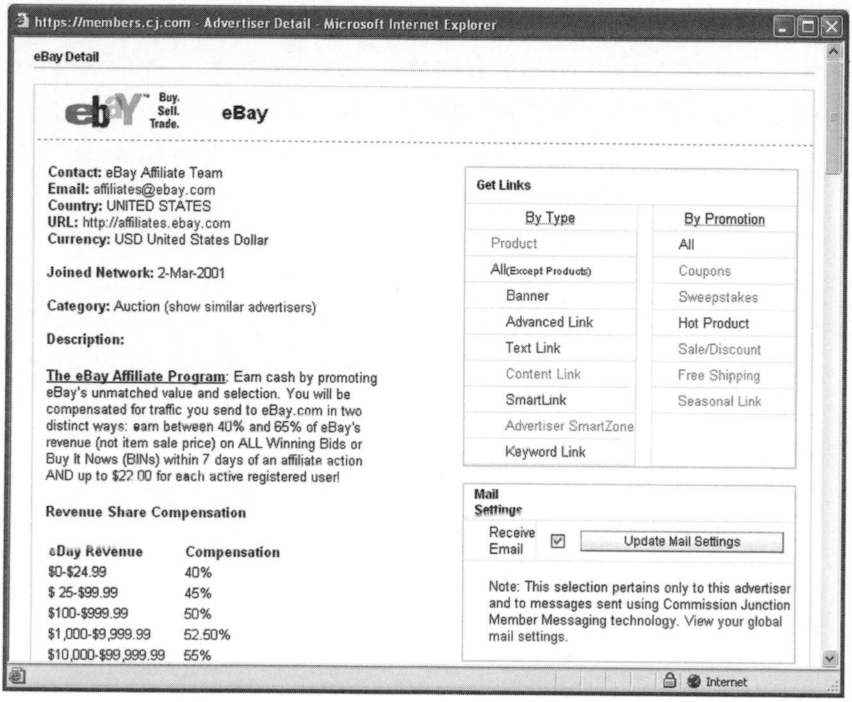

regarding the commissions and referral periods. In eBay's case, you are offered a twofold commission structure, one that pays commissions on a revenue-sharing basis and one that pays commissions based on the number of active registered users (ACRUs) your ads generate. Both commission structures have performance tiers that allow you to earn higher commissions if you generate more revenue or more ACRUs.

Another important consideration is the Get Links section in the upper right portion of the Advertiser Detail page. Here you will find hyperlinks to each of the different kinds of links the advertiser (in this case eBay) offers. If you own a web site of your own, you might use any number of these links—and I would encourage you to explore them—but as a search marketer, your primary concern is to make sure that the Keyword Link type is active (blue). This informs you that search marketing is allowed. If the Keyword Link type is not active, you may not be able to advertise that affiliate program directly on search engines— although you can always e-mail Commission Junction or the advertiser for clarification.

Finally, to join the program you must scroll through the Advertiser Detail page, reading and accepting any special terms and conditions that may apply, and then clicking on Accept at the bottom of the page. Some advertisers will accept you immediately; some may deny you immediately; others may take hours or even days to review your application.

Once you are approved, you will need to return to the Advertiser Detail page and click on the Keyword Link hyperlink in order to continue. This will open the Keyword Link page (see Figure 5.5).

On the right-hand side of the Keyword Link page, click Get HTML to take yourself to the Get HTML page shown in Figure 5.6. *Pay special attention* to the Usage Recommendation, Protected Keywords, and Non-compete Keywords when you place your ads for this program in the next chapter. Any violation of the affiliate program's keyword policy could result in nonpayment of commissions, meaning you will have spent money running ads and will earn nothing in return.

At the bottom of the page is the tracking code you will need to use as your destination when you create your ads in the next chapter. This code will direct those who click on your ads to the eBay home page and will also alert eBay to the fact that it was you who sent them (thus eBay can track the results to determine your commission). You may select this code and copy it yourself. Alternatively, you can click on the Highlight Code / Copy Code button to

Figure 5.5 Keyword Link Page
Source: Commission Junction

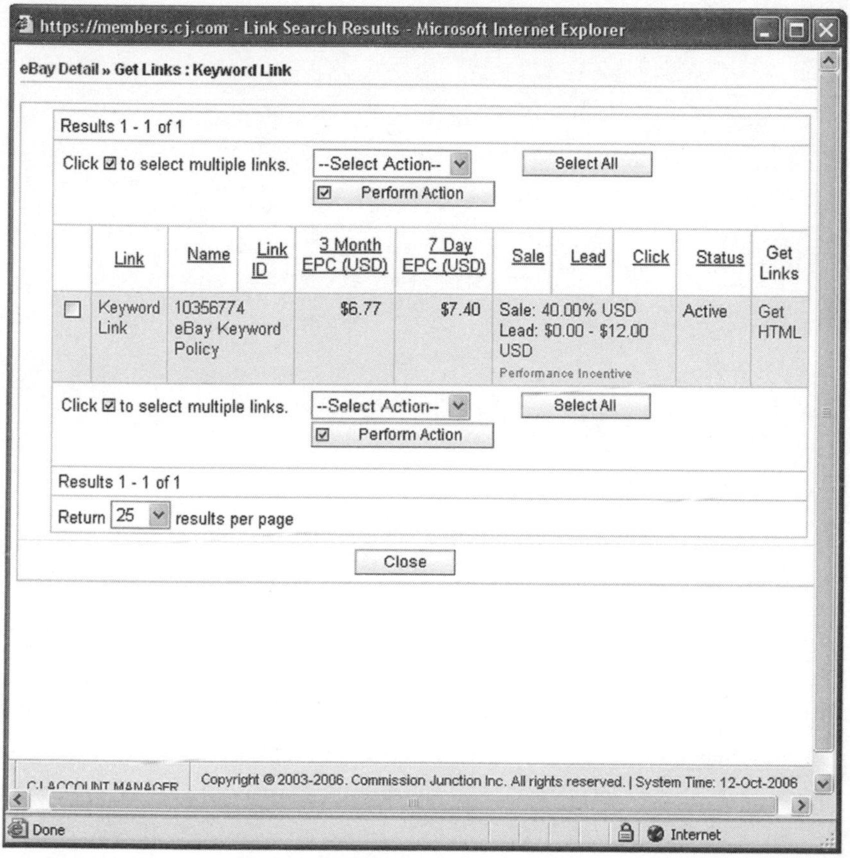

copy it automatically. Either way, you will then paste the tracking code—making sure to label which affiliate program the code is for—in a document and save it to use when you create your ads in Chapter 6.

CAUTION: Please do not use the tracking code in the example in Figure 5.6. You want to generate this code yourself, so that Commission Junction can embed it with your own PID. If you use the code in Figure 5.6, you will not earn commissions.

Figure 5.6 Get HTML Page
Source: Commission Junction

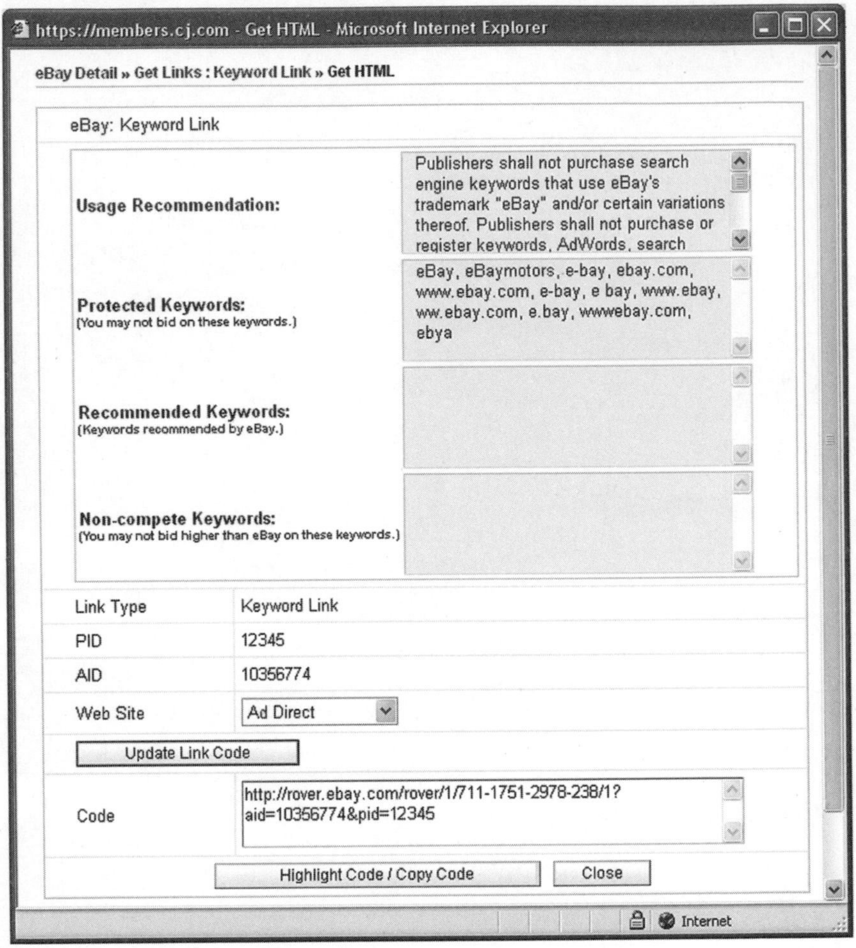

Now that you have your tracking code saved, you are ready to start signing up with search engines and running ads. You can skip ahead to Chapter 6 if you'd like to start running ads right away, or you can continue on with this chapter to learn how to get your tracking code from Amazon as well.

> **TIP:** In addition to the standard keyword link code, which wi
> directly to eBay's home page, eBay also has what it calls the Flexible
> Destination Tool. This tool enables you to create customized tracking
> codes directing potential customers to any eBay page you wish to send
> them. This can be especially useful if you run ads for baby cribs or
> used autos, as you can link your ad directly to a relevant results page
> on eBay instead of just sending your targeted traffic to eBay's home
> page. Be sure to experiment with the Flexible Destination Tool, as it will
> dramatically improve your conversion rate. The link to the Affiliate
> Toolkit is http://affiliates.ebay.com/tools/.

Amazon.com's Associates Central

Amazon may be only one affiliate program, but the advertising opportunities are enormous. Along with one of the largest and most varied inventories on the Internet, Amazon is one of the most recognized and trusted brands on the Web. Its affiliate program is also one of the largest on the Web and, as you are about to find out, one of the friendliest and easiest to use. After logging on to Associates Central (https://affiliate-program.amazon.com) with the e-mail address and password you provided during the registration process, you'll be taken to the Associates Central home page shown in Figure 5.7.

From here, you'll click on "Build Links" on the left side menu and then click on "Text Links" that appears beneath it. This will bring you to the Text Links page shown in Figure 5.8, where you will be able to build three different types of text links, all of which you will find quite useful as a search marketer.

The Text Links page offers three different types of links you can generate: Link to Favorite Destinations, Link to Search Results, and Link to Any Page at Amazon.

Figure 5.7   Associates Central Home Page
Source: Amazon.com

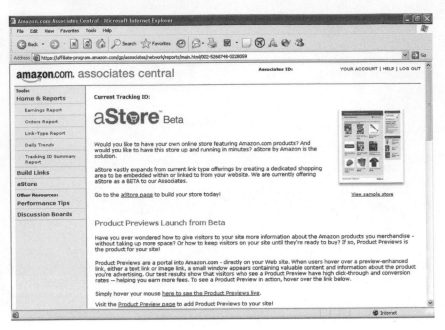

Link to Favorite Destinations. Link to Favorite Destinations allows you to choose a landing page at Amazon.com that displays certain product lines and subcategories. If you select Baby from the Select Product Line drop-down, for instance, and Strollers from the Select a Subcategory drop-down and click Get HTML, you'll be taken to the screen shown in Figure 5.9.

On this screen, you'll find the tracking code for the text link you've created. This code is designed to be added to a Web page, however, so you will need to copy only the portion of the code I've highlighted in Figure 5.9, which consists of everything inside the quotation marks after the "href=" portion of the code. When you use this portion of the code as the destination link for the ad you will create in Chapter 6, it will lead to the page shown in Figure 5.10.

Figure 5.8 Text Links Page
Source: Amazon.com

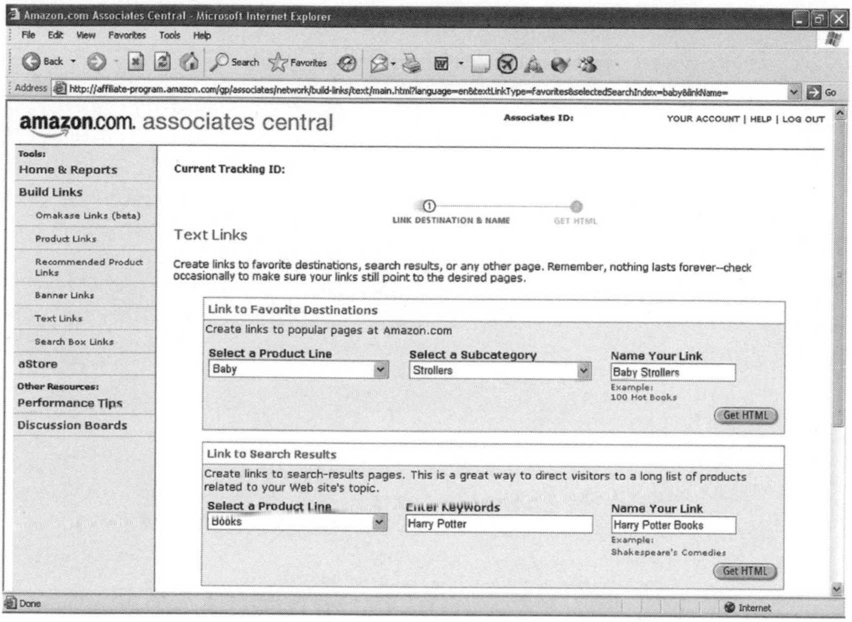

Link to Search Results. Link to Search Results allows you to link to a search results page on Amazon.com by selecting a product line (or you can select to search All Products) and keywords for the search. If you select All Products from the product line drop-down, for instance, and enter Harry Potter in the Enter Keywords box and click Get HTML, you'll be taken to the screen shown in Figure 5.11.

Once again, you'll find the tracking code for the text link you've created. This code is also designed to be added to a Web page, so you will need to copy the portion of the code I've high-lighted in Figure 5.11. As before, this consists of everything inside the quotation marks after the "href=" portion of the code. If you use this portion of the code as the destination link for an ad you place on Google or another search engine, it will lead to the page shown in Figure 5.12.

Figure 5.9 Favorite Destinations Tracking Link
Source: Amazon.com

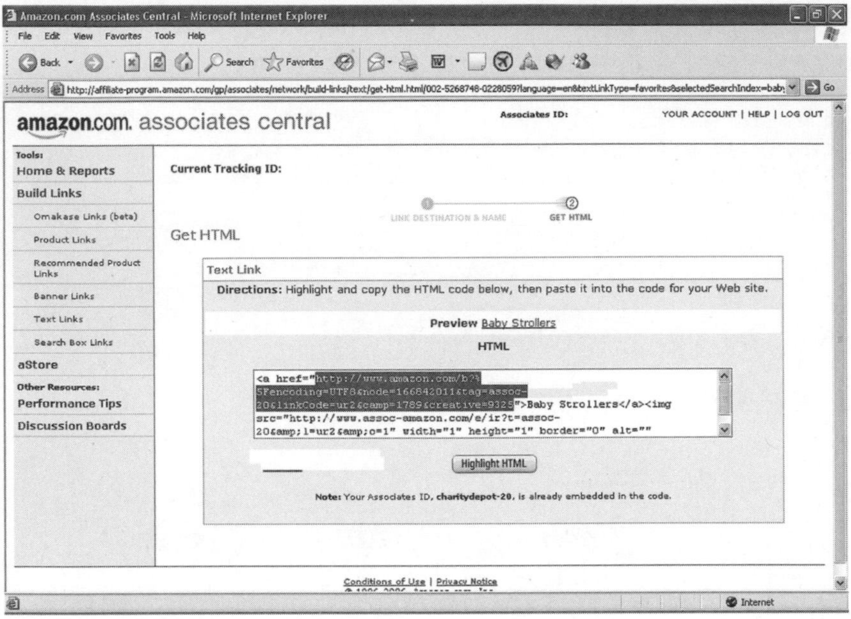

You might notice that because we selected All Products when building this search results link, we do not see only Harry Potter books or only Harry Potter movies. Instead we see a mixture of products lines relating to Harry Potter.

Link to Any Page at Amazon.com. Link to Any Page at Amazon.com allows you to link to any page on Amazon.com (except search results pages) by copying the URL for that page into the Enter the URL field. Then simply click on Get HTML. As in the last two examples, copy everything inside the quotation marks after the "href=" portion of the code. When you paste this portion of the code into the destination link of the ads you create, it will lead to the same Amazon URL you pasted into the Link to Any

Figure 5.10 Baby Strollers Landing Page
Source: Amazon.com

Figure 5.11 Link to Search Results Tracking Link
Source: Amazon.com

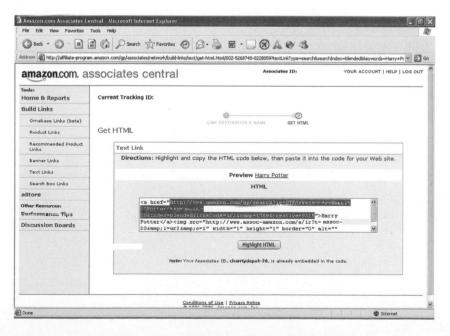

Figure 5.12 Harry Potter Search Results Page
Source: Amazon.com

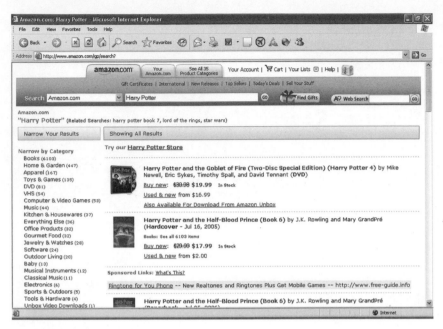

Page tool, only now it will be embedded with the tracking code necessary for you to earn commissions on purchases.

Now that you have joined some affiliate networks, selected some affiliate programs, and generated some HTML tracking code to embed in your ads, you are finally ready to bring it all together and start your first search marketing campaigns. In the next chapter, I'll walk you through the process of signing up with Google, and creating your first campaigns.

Chapter 6

Creating Search Marketing Campaigns

This is the chapter where it all really starts to come together. You've learned some basics about both affiliate advertising and search marketing. You have joined some affiliate networks and selected some affiliate programs to promote. You've even obtained the tracking code you will need to embed in your ads so your clients can track the actions of the customers you send to them and, of course, keep track of your commissions. Now you can finally start building advertising campaigns and promoting your affiliate programs.

First I teach you how to write effective ad copy. Then I explain how to choose relevant keywords and key phrases to trigger your ads. After that, I give you some tips about deciding how much to bid and how to set your campaign's daily budget. Once you've learned all this, I walk you step-by-step through the process of joining both Google and MSN and setting up your first campaigns.

What do you say we get started?

STEPS TO CREATE A CAMPAIGN

Before you set up our first real campaign, let's discuss the steps involved and the principles you'll use to make your decisions. Then you will be ready to create your first campaign.

Campaignwide Settings

There is some variation from one search engine to another in the campaign settings and at which stage in the process you will be required to set them. Most search engines have some version of the following setting, however.

Basic Settings. The basic campaign settings will include the name of the campaign, a start and end date, and sometimes even specific times the campaign will or will not run.

Target Audience. When you create a new campaign, you must specify which language or languages your target audience speaks and which countries and/or regions you wish your ads to appear in. Some search engines, like Google for instance, allow finer-grained geo-targeting tools that provide you with such flexibility as entering an address and running ads within a 10-mile radius of that address. This is a useful function if, for instance, you own a flower shop with a delivery range of 10 miles and do not want your ads to run outside that range.

Budget Options. Here you will specify exactly how much you are willing to spend per day or month on this campaign and whether you want to spread your exposure evenly or use up your budget as quickly as possible. We talk about how to choose the right budget amount after discussing the bidding process, as this is typically the point in the process where you would also set a new campaign's budget or adjust an existing campaign's budget. Be aware, though, that although many search engines represent this amount as a daily budget, if you look closely you will find that they are really committing to a monthly budget, calculated based on the daily limit you enter.

Networks. Many search engines have search networks, other search pages that use a bigger search engine as the back end for their search results, and content networks as well. When you create a campaign, you will need to specify whether you want your ads to run on these networks. I highly recommend that you participate in the search networks, but choosing whether to participate in content networks is a more difficult decision.

Generally, I have noticed higher costs per click and lower returns per click on content networks compared to search networks. Sometimes you have a small profit margin to work with; other times you do not. I have had only one really successful campaign that relied heavily on content network traffic, but this was worth tens of thousands of dollars to me over the life of the campaign, so I have to say that there can sometimes be rewards to participating in content networks.

My advice, however, is to save them for later. In the beginning, the tighter margins you are likely to encounter will only serve to make the tough job of becoming profitable in this game a little bit tougher.

Advanced Options. Almost all search engines offer a few unusual options for fine-tuning your campaign. Some may be more useful than others, but I would say that none are for beginners, and I cannot recommend any such options to anyone just getting started. After you are established in the business and are well aware of the strengths and weaknesses of your own campaigns, you will be your own best judge regarding which of these tools might be of some assistance to you.

Writing Effective Ads

As I've said before, ad copy is *king*. The text you write for your search marketing ads is the most important piece of this puzzle, and your ability to produce good ad copy will ultimately decide your fate in this business. A turn of phrase can make the difference between impressions that turn into clicks and clicks that turn into purchases. Because of the performance-based search algorithms used by Google and others, when you write a better ad, you lower your costs and raise your volume at the same time. That's the best way to get an edge over your competition.

Keep four things in mind as you write your ads:

1. Use ad grouping.
2. What are you promoting?
3. Why should your targets get it from you?
4. What do you need them to do?

Use Ad Grouping. Ad groups are sets of ads and keywords within a campaign grouped by relevance. For instance, you don't want to write an Amazon ad for toys and an Amazon ad for college textbooks and have both ads showing the keyword *children's toys* because both are grouped together and share the same keyword list. Within your Amazon campaign, you will need an ad group for toys (maybe even multiple ad groups for multiple toys and toy categories) and an ad group for college textbooks. This way, you can create separate relevant keyword lists for each distinct ad group.

What Are You Promoting? The headline of your ad should clearly indicate what you are promoting, and the destination link of your ad should take the user as quickly as possible to the point of sale. For example, if you are trying to sell a Canon PowerShot DSC 600, not only should this be the ad's headline, but you should be certain that the landing page your ad directs users to offers the product for sale. If the landing page is cluttered with a number of other cameras, or if the user needs to search further to find the specific product, you are much less likely to get a sale than if you send the user to a page dedicated to ordering the Canon PowerShot DSC 600.

Conversely, if you are promoting an entire line of digital cameras, your headline and ad text should be appropriately broad. You should also make sure that your landing page offers a broad selection of digital cameras. I'll provide some specific examples later, when we build our first campaigns.

Why Should Your Targets Get It from You? What can you offer customers to entice them to procure the product or service from you? The first line of your ad's description is a great place to highlight low prices, sales, discounts, wide selection, or sometimes even just having a hard-to-find item in stock. Does the affiliate program you're promoting offer free downloads? Free shipping? If the word *free* is applicable in some way, it is a great click booster. But keep in mind, you want to use it only when it is appropriate. If you can't deliver on what you promised, or if the free product or service isn't tied to your commission somehow, you may deliver—and pay for—an enormous number of clicks, but generate few or no commissions in return.

What Do You Need Them to Do? If users must register with a site for you to earn your commission, or if they must pay a membership fee to participate, don't fail to mention this in your ad. Disclosing that there is a registration process customers must go through will reduce the number of clicks you receive—and pay for, remember—but you are weeding out people who wouldn't have registered anyway. Why pay for clicks that won't earn commissions? If your conversion rate is higher, this should more than offset the burden of a lower click-through rate.

You are free to put a positive spin on this in your ad, of course. The second line of your description could read, for instance, "Low Membership Fees" or "Free & Easy Online Registration," but be sure to let them know.

Also keep in mind that proper grammar and sentence structure might not always make for the most effective ad when you are working with such limited space. Occasionally, abbreviations will give you the extra few spaces you need to complete a more effective sales pitch. Grammatical errors such as capitalizing the first letter of certain words in the middle of the sentence can add emphasis where you want it and when you would otherwise be unable to. Using your search terms in the heading and text of the ad can also improve performance. Very small differences sometimes set one ad apart from another and make the crucial difference between two similar ads.

Select Your Keywords

Keywords are the search terms you want that will trigger the display of your ads when search engine users enter them into a search. Choosing relevant keywords for your ads is critical to their success. An ad for a specific product will likely be most successful if runs only when the user is searching for that specific product, so a very narrow list of keywords can be important. An ad for a range of products, however, will require a broader list of keywords to really succeed. You will find as you progress that successful ads focusing on individual products will have wider profit margins but a lower overall volume of click traffic, whereas successful ads with a broader focus will have tighter profit margins but will generate higher volume.

Selecting Keywords for Narrowly Focused Ads. The narrowly focused keyword selection process for ads promoting specific items is fairly simple. If you are promoting the Canon PowerShot DSC 600, you would certainly choose "Canon PowerShot DSC 600," "Canon DSC 600," "PowerShot DSC 600," "PowerShot DSC 600," and "DSC 600." You might also purchase "Canon PowerShot" or "PowerShot," although if your landing page markets only the DSC 600, you might get better margins and performance from an ad for the whole Canon PowerShot line of digital cameras, directing consumers to a landing page featuring most or all of the PowerShot product line. You would not bid on "Canon" or "Digital Cameras," as your ad and landing page for the Canon PowerShot DSC 600 might not appeal to a large portion of users who search for digital cameras, and, as a result, your ad would perform poorly in comparison to other ads more broadly tailored to a search for digital cameras.

Selecting Keywords for Broadly Focused Ads. The broadly focused keyword selection process for ads promoting a brand line or a whole product market—say digital cameras, for instance—is much more complex. Rather than spending hours brainstorming, trying to come up with dozens, or even hundreds, of appropriate keywords, I recommend using a keyword selection tool of some kind. Most search engines, including Google, offer such a tool. By entering in a word or phrase, like *digital cameras*, you will receive a list of sometimes hundreds of related keywords. Please do not attempt to use them all without reviewing them first. Many will be less relevant than you would hope, and some may be far too specific for your broadly focused ad. But if you slowly go down the list, deciding which words and phrases are appropriate and which are not, you will have built a comprehensive keyword list in a fraction of the time it would take to think of them all on your own.

> **TIP:** If you are looking for a professional version of a keyword suggestion tool, Wordtracker (www.wordtracker.com) goes well beyond the tools currently provided by Google AdWords and its competitors. Wordtracker collects actual search terms that have been submitted to not one but a collection of multiple search engines through the search service called Dogpile (www.dogpile.com). Dogpile lets users conduct searches on many different search engines at the same time. Its database of 340 million search queries is available to Wordtracker users, and when you receive results, they are ranked by how frequently they appeared in search engine queries in the recent past.

It can be hard work to set up large numbers of narrowly focused ad groups, and you might have to set up dozens before they collectively approach the volume level of a single broadly focused ad, but the higher margins might be worth the extra effort. If you concentrate on broadly focused ads, the volume will be much easier to generate, but narrower margins might mean little or no actual profit. There is a way, though, that you can sometimes have your cake and eat it too.

A few search engines (Google is one of them) offer an often overlooked feature that allows you to dynamically insert keywords into your ad text and, even more important, your destination link. "What does this mean?" you might ask. This means that you can write a broad-appeal ad and use the keyword insertion function to customize that ad to match the search terms the user entered, making it appear as narrowly focused as needed to attract the user's attention. Even better, you can customize the destination link—with some affiliate programs—to dynamically pass the search terms along to the affiliate site, so it can serve up exactly what the user was searching for in the first place. By writing a single ad and collecting a much looser selection of keywords into a single ad group, you can get much of the benefit of narrowly focused ads without the labor-intensive process of creating dozens (or more) of ad groups. I give an example later in the chapter when we set up our first campaigns.

Keyword Matching Options

Of course, just selecting your keywords isn't all you need to worry about. Each keyword you select also needs a matching option. There are four basic types, though sometimes search engines call them by different names. They are *broad match, phrase match, exact match,* and *negative match.*

Broad Match. A broad match designation means that if your keyword or keywords appear anywhere in the search terms used, your ad will be considered for display on the results page. If *yankee* is on your ad's keyword list, then your ad might show up in a search for "Yankee baseball cards," but your ad might also show up in a search for Mark Twain's *A Connecticut Yankee in King Arthur's Court.* You can see how using broad match could hurt your efforts to display your ad only in front of the most relevant audience possible.

However, if you believe the overwhelming majority of searches using your keyword are in fact relevant, you could safely use broad match, along with a just few negative match keywords to weed out the irrelevant searches. I talk about negative match in a minute.

Phrase Match. The phrase *match designation* means that if your keywords appear, in order, anywhere in the search terms used, your ad will be considered for display on the results page. For instance, if your phrase matched keywords are "Pittsburgh bus schedule," your ad might appear in the results for a search of "find Pittsburgh bus schedule," but it would not appear in the search results for "When is Jerome 'the Bus' Bettis scheduled to return to Pittsburgh?" If you use broad match, your ad might appear in both search results.

Exact Match. This designation means that your ad will be considered for display on the results page only if your keyword or words exactly match the search terms. If you choose to use exact match for the keyword phrase, "Used Atari 5200," your ad would not display in a search for "Find used Atari 5200." I'm not a big fan of exact match, generally speaking, but you might find some use for it. As a search marketer, I believe that broad or phrase match combined with some negative keywords is probably almost always going to work better than exact match.

Negative Match. This match type is a little different than the others in that it affects all the other keywords in your ad group (or campaign, if you use campaign-level negative match). Any word you add to your keyword list with a negative match designation will cause any other keyword in your list not to trigger your ads if the search term also includes the negative keyword. If you have an ad for baseball equipment and one of your keywords is "bats," for instance, then adding "vampire" as a negative keyword would help you avoid showing your ad to uninterested horror film aficionados, which would probably lower your click-through rate.

Some search engines, like Google, will use broad match by default, while others default to exact match. Either way, you need to decide for yourself which matching option is right for each keyword and keyword phrase. I provide some examples later in the chapter when we actually build some campaigns.

Bidding on Keywords

Adding a keyword to your ad group does not guarantee that your ad or ads will always be shown when that keyword is used in a search query. In fact, when you are advertising affiliate programs, chances are that several other search marketers are promoting the same program you are and will often select many of the same keywords as you. Your ads will have to compete with everyone else's for position and for number of impressions (each time an ad is shown is an *impression*). Part of that competition is bidding. If you are willing to pay more than your competition, your ad will have a better chance of being shown more often—and in a better position.

On some search engines, the bidding process is all that determines who wins and who loses, but with the performance-based search engines I recommend, there is another factor: ad performance, as measured by your click-through rate (CTR). As I mentioned in Chapter 3, an ad with a higher CTR may appear more often and in a better position than an ad with a lower CTR, without necessarily costing you more. The bottom line, though, is that you do have to pay something, especially to get an ad started, and once you've created your ads and chosen your keywords, you will have to bid on those keywords to let Google or another search engine know just how much you are willing to pay for each click your ad generates.

You can bid on individual keywords or use a default bid for an entire ad group. Theoretically, bidding on each keyword individual could allow you to optimize your return for every keyword you use. Of course, you would have to track the performance of each of those keywords individually and calculate your return per click (RPC) and total return on each keyword separately to determine the optimal bid amounts. In practice, this is not very practical, and even with special software that's available online to help streamline the process, you still have to do a lot of the work yourself. The bottom line is, if you organize your ad groups carefully and the keywords they contain are similar in both relevance and focus (broad or narrow), then by setting your bids at the ad group level you will avoid the nightmare of tracking every keyword's performance, and it should have very little negative impact on your actual earnings.

Finding the perfect bid amount is a subject I discuss in Chapter 9. For now, let's concentrate on deciding what our initial bid should be. If you recall, Commission Junction's Advertiser List page included some columns called "3 Month EPC" and "7 Day EPC." These are the gross earnings per hundred clicks, and most affiliate networks offer a similar statistic for each of their affiliate programs. If you assume your return will be somewhere near average—keeping in mind a very good or very bad ad could be much higher or lower—you might safely bid [1//100] of either of these EPCs (remember, the affiliate networks report EPC as earnings per hundred clicks). If, for example, the EPC is 4.87 cents $(4.87/100 = 0.0487$, or roughly 5 cents), a conservative bid would start at either 4 or 5 cents. Cautious (or aggressive) bidders might start a little lower (or higher) depending on their comfort level, perhaps trusting more in their budget maximum to protect against a dramatic financial loss.

I myself will often bid twice the average return. I do this to more quickly obtain results on which to base future bid adjustment (again, see Chapter 9, "Performance Monitoring and Tuning") and also because I have begun to trust in my ability to produce returns that are, in fact, much higher than the average returns. I do not recommend you start like this, but if you meet with some success, you may begin to set your initial bids more aggressively over time.

I will walk you through actually setting these bids very soon now, when we set up our first campaigns, but first we have one last subject to discuss. Namely, setting our daily budget.

Budget Maximums

A *budget maximum* is a limit on the amount of money you can spend in a particular period of time, such as a month or a day. The first rule when setting your budget is to not budget more than you are actually willing to lose. Some ads do perform well right out of the gate in terms of click-through rate and volume, but that does not mean they will convert well and earn commissions for you. It is entirely possible to spend thousands of dollars in a few short hours and then discover later that you generated no commissions whatsoever.

In fact, it has happened to me, and the experience almost caused me to quit the business altogether, just weeks before I began to strike it rich. Don't let a similar mistake push you out of the business too early. Set your budget high enough to generate some traffic to analyze, but never set it higher than the amount you are actually prepared to spend. In the beginning, think of an ad budget as a sort of safety valve. It's a limit you set in case an ad really takes off before you even know whether it can earn back what you spend on it. Once an ad proves it can earn you more money per click than it costs per click to run it, go ahead and open up that valve as wide as you like—or can afford. But with a new and unproven campaign, use that safety valve to protect yourself.

Don't forget what I told you before: What most search engines refer to as a *daily budget* is really just a figure used to calculate a monthly budget. The figure you enter for a daily budget can be exceeded, even doubled or tripled, on any given day as long as by the end of the month the daily *average* is below your maximum. This isn't something that will happen very often to you, if at all, but you should still be cautious and keep a close eye on new campaigns.

Don't worry if you are still wondering, "But how do I actually do all this?" It's finally time to start a real search campaign, and now I am going to walk you through the actual steps with both Google and MSN. By the end of this chapter, your first search campaigns will be up and running.

JOIN GOOGLE ADWORDS AND CREATE A CAMPAIGN

I'll start with the AdWords program, as Google is one of the largest and easiest-to-use search and content networks on the Web. To sign up for AdWords, simply visit its home page at http://adwords.google.com (see Figure 6.1).

AdWords Home Page

The sign-up process is tied very tightly into the process for setting up your first campaign and ad group, as you will see in a moment. I will let you know when you are working on your first campaign and when you are simply selecting accountwide settings.

Sign Up Now. The AdWords home page is frequently updated, but it always prominently features a "Sign up now" button somewhere on the page, in this case on the upper right-hand side. If you already have a Google account, you can sign into AdWords using your existing user name and password, but for this example I will assume you are new to Google and walk you through the process of signing up as well. Click on "Sign up now" to

Figure 6.1 AdWords Home Page
Source: Screenshots © Google Inc. and are used with permission.

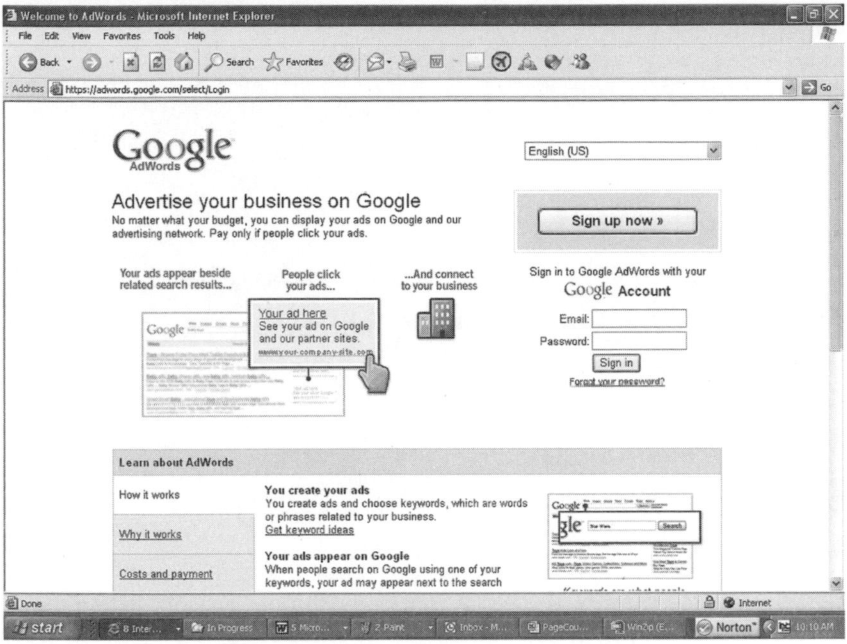

begin, and you will be taken immediately to the Choose Edition page (see Figure 6.2).

Choose Edition

Here you must select from one of two choices.

1. *Starter Edition.* The Starter Edition is for advertisers advertising a single product or service. Google recommends it for those who are new to Internet advertising, and you can move up to the Standard Edition at any time.
2. *Standard Edition.* The Standard Edition offers Google's full range of AdWords features and functionality, and Google recommends it for experienced Internet advertisers and medium- or large-sized businesses.

Figure 6.2 Choose Edition Page
Source: Screenshots © Google Inc. and are used with permission.

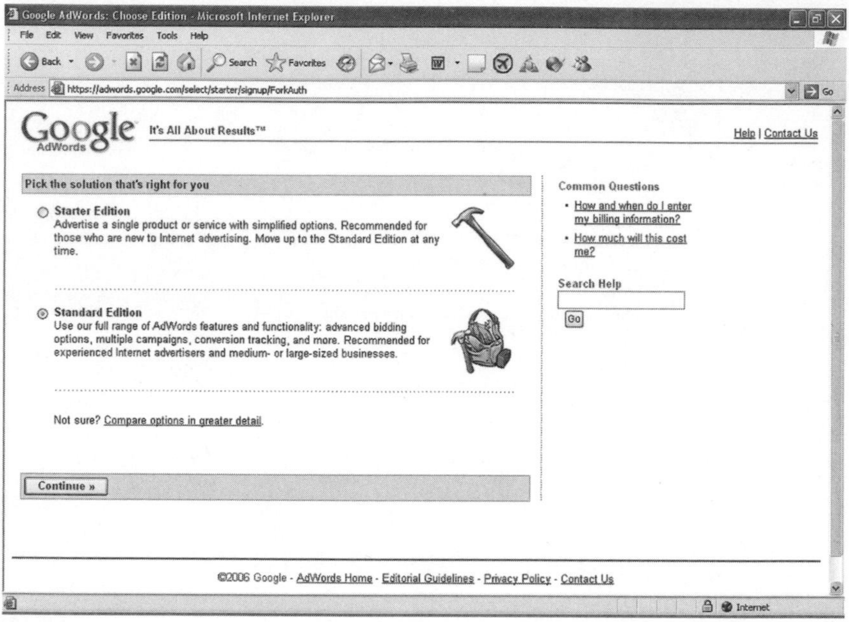

As an affiliate advertiser, you will be starting a number of campaigns for various different affiliate programs, so you should select the Standard Edition before clicking Continue, which will bring you to the Identify Customers page (see Figure 6.3).

Identify Customers

The Identify Customers page is actually the start of setting up your first campaign, so be aware as you fill it out that you will want to choose the languages and locations that are appropriate for the affiliate program you have decided to join. In this example, I use eBay's affiliate program for the United States.

Target Customers by Language. Here you will select the language or languages your target customers speak.

Figure 6.3 Identify Customers Page
Source: Screenshots © Google Inc. and are used with permission.

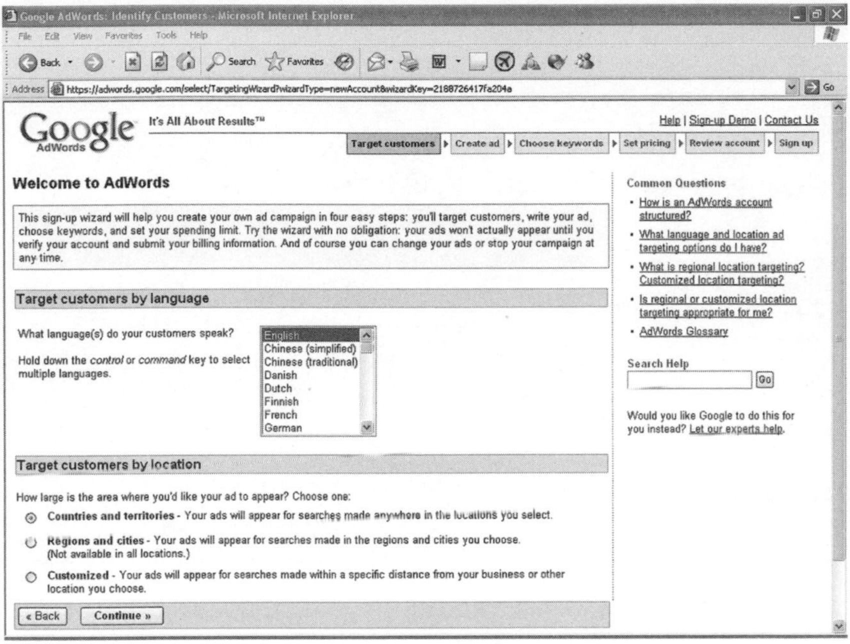

Target Customers by Location. Here you will decide to target your customers by country and territories, regions and cities, or choose a customized area within a certain radius of a location you choose.

For eBay's affiliate program, I select "English" and "Countries and territories." Make the appropriate selections for your own affiliate program, and click Continue to go to the second Identify Customers page (see Figure 6.4).

Target Customers by Country or Territory. Here you may select one or more countries or territories and click on Add to add them to the "Selected Countries and/or Territories" box. When you are finished, click Continue to go to the Create Ad page (see Figure 6.5).

Figure 6.4   Second Identify Customers Page
Source: Screenshots © Google Inc. and are used with permission.

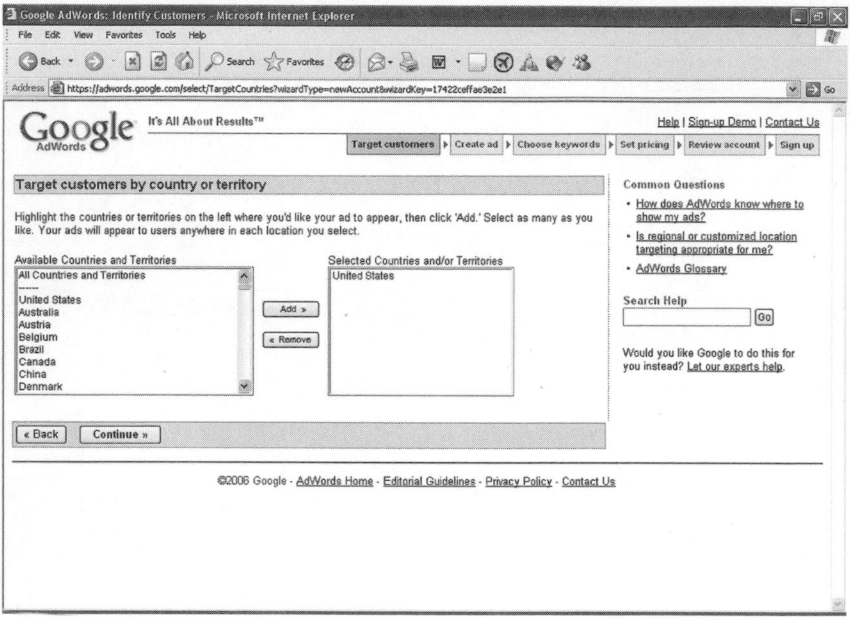

Create Ad

The Create Ad page is where we build our first ad. There are five components to these four-line ads, as you can see in Figure 6.5.

Headline. The ad headline may be up to 25 characters long and should appropriately represent what you believe the searcher is looking for based on the keywords you plan to bid on. This ad is a broadly focused ad, and I will probably be bidding on keywords like "shop" or "shopping." Notice that I have entered "Shop on eBay" as my headline. If I am planning on bidding on a few different keywords, I might also try using the keyword insertion tool to customize my heading to match the user's search terms that triggered my ad. Figure 6.6 is an example of the keyword insertion tool used in the headline.

Figure 6.5 Create Ad Page
Source: Screenshots © Google Inc. and are used with permission.

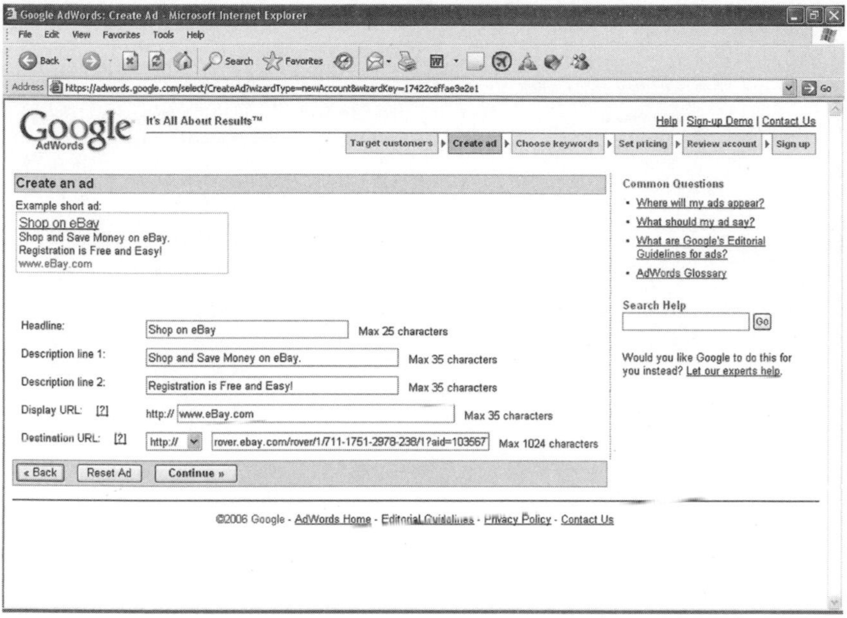

Now, if I bid on the phrase "shop and save," for instance, my headline would appear to the user as "Shop and save on eBay."

You should also be aware that there are a few different formats to the keyword insertion tool. If I had not capitalized {keyword: . . . }, then it would read, "shop and save on eBay" without capitalizing the first word. If I had capitalized the K and W {Key-Word: . . . }, then my ad would have read, "Shop And Save on eBay," with each word of the keyword phrase capitalized. Note that the full keyword insertion code includes the word *shopping*. This will be the default word used in the headline should the search term be unable to display due to the length or for any other reason.

Description Line 1. In the first line of the description, I usually expand on the headline with a reason or reasons for the user to

Figure 6.6 Example of the Keyword Insertion Tool Used in the Headline
Source: Screenshots © Google Inc. and are used with permission.

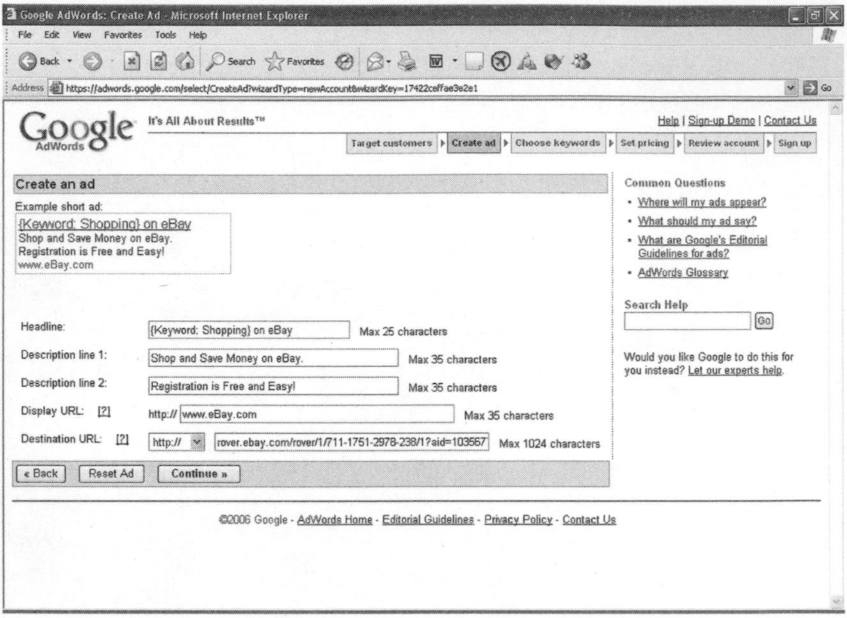

go to the site I'm promoting. In this instance, I have typed, "Shop and Save Money on eBay." My goal here is to suggest that by going to eBay instead of clicking on some other site's ad, the user might save money, which is certainly possible for a savvy bidder on eBay. I might also have suggested it would be easy to find what the user wants on eBay. The point is, in this line of your ad you should give the user a reason to choose this site over the others.

Description line 2. The second line of the description can sometimes be used in the same way as the first, giving the user a second reason to visit the site. I prefer, however, to use this line—when appropriate—to weed out traffic that will not earn a commission anyway. Since eBay requires users to register to use the service, and because these registrations are the bulk of my revenue, I try to let users know that registration will be necessary. This way, people who are not willing to register don't waste their time—and my money—by clicking on my ad. Of course, I do try to put a positive spin on it, hence the phrase, "Registration is Free and Easy!" Note also the use of an exclamation point. Punctuation, if used intelligently, can often improve your ad's CTR, but be aware that AdWords will not allow you to overuse it.

Display URL. This is the URL that your ad will display. It does not have to match the Destination URL, but they both must point—eventually—to the same top-level domain.

Destination URL. This is the actual URL you want customers to go to when they click on your ad, and here is where you will enter the tracking code you generated in Chapter 5 when you signed up for eBay (or whatever other program you may have chosen). By the way, all Commission Junction affiliate programs allow you to uniquely identify your ads using a Shopper ID (SID). This optional variable can be inserted into the tracking code to individually track the actions of each and every customer who clicks on one of your ads, but I typically use it just to separately identify each ad group so that I can calculate my returns by ad group later. If I intend to name this ad group eBay Shopping, for instance, I would add the following piece of code to the end of my tracking code: &SID=ebayshopping.

In Chapter 7, I explain how this SID will help you separately calculate the commission earnings of specific ad groups so you can determine which ad groups are profitable.

Once you have finished filling in the five elements of your ad, click Continue to go on to the Choose Keywords page (Figure 6.7). Be aware that Google will quickly review your ad and may reject

Figure 6.7   Choose Keywords Page
Source: Screenshots © Google Inc. and are used with permission.

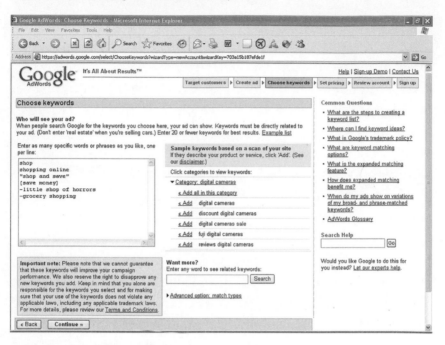

any portion of it that violates Google's editorial guidelines. Goo-gle always provides clear explanations for these rejections, and you will not have any problem understanding what you've done and how to fix it if such a rejection occurs. Be aware that you can also apply for an exception if you feel Google's policy was not cor-rectly applied in any particular case, in which case an AdWords representative will review your ad manually.

Choose Keywords

Here you will select your keywords. Don't bother using the ones I listed previously. I picked a few barely relevant keywords and phrases, as well as some negative keywords, just as examples. I do not use actual keywords that have worked well for me as exam-ples. A few thousand readers all bidding on the same keywords and running the same ads would be a surefire way to ruin my business, so you will have to find good keywords on your own. If you happen to pick some of my own best keywords and phrases to trigger your ads, then good luck, and may the best ads win.

Choose Keywords. I will not repeat my descriptions of keyword matching types here that I made early in this chapter, but I will tell you the formats for each of these matching types on Google.

- *Broad match.* Any keyword or keywords entered without quotes, brackets, or hyphens.
- *Phrase match.* Any keyword or keywords entered within quotes.
- *Exact match.* Any keyword or keywords entered within brackets.
- *Negative match.* Any keyword or keywords entered after a hyphen.

You can see clearly in the preceding example which keywords are intended for broad match, phrase match, and exact match, as well as which keywords and phrases are intended as negative matches to avoid triggering my ad for an irrelevant search.

When you are finished entering your keywords, click Continue to move on to the Set Pricing page.

Set Pricing

The Set Pricing page is where I start bidding on the keywords in my ad group, setting my campaign's budget, and using Google's traffic estimator tool for the first time (see Figure 6.8).

Choose a Currency. This is an accountwide setting, not part of the individual campaign we have been working on. This is where

Figure 6.8 Set Pricing Page
Source: Screenshots © Google Inc. and are used with permission.

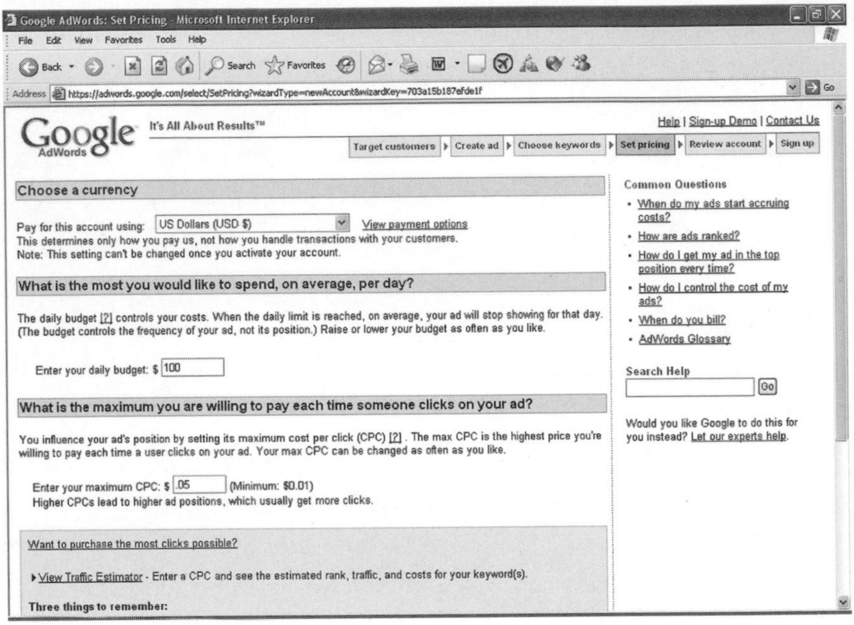

you designate which currency you will use to bid on, budget for, and pay for these ads.

What Is the Most You Would Like to Spend, on Average, per Day? This is your daily budget, but remember, Google will guarantee only that this budget will not be exceeded *on average* by the end of the month. I have entered $100, but when setting your initial budgets, this amount is dependent entirely on your working capital and comfort level.

What Is the Maximum You Are Willing to Pay Each Time Someone Clicks on Your Ad? This is the amount you are bidding per click for all the keywords in your ad group. I have set my initial bid at 5 cents, based on the three-month EPC (earnings per hundred clicks) of $4.07 for the eBay affiliate program at the time I was setting up this campaign, at which time the average returns were roughly 4 cents. My 5-cent bid, then, is very moderately aggressive, but I hope to do better than average, and I am likely to pay at least a little less than my maximum bid anyway.

You can also set individual bids for each keyword, but I do not recommend it, as this will require you to track individual results as well. In the rare instance when you might wish to set a separate bid for an individual keyword, I would set up a separate ad group as well, so that the keyword has its own ad, with its own SID to track results. Be sure, however, that your keywords for each ad group are very similar in both relevance and focus (broad or narrow), or a single bid amount will not work very well.

View Traffic Estimator. Traffic estimators are not terribly accurate, as they can only guess at what your ad's performance might be against the keywords entered, but they can give you a rough idea of whether or not your daily budget might be reached or whether your maximum bid is below the minimum amount required by certain high-volume keywords as you start to bid. Go ahead and take a quick peek, but don't expect your own traffic to closely approximate these estimates. Most often it will be a bit off.

When you are finished, click Continue to go to the Review Your Selections page (see Figure 6.9).

Review Your Selections

Simply review your selections, editing any that might not be exactly what you intended them to be, before clicking on the Continue to Sign Up button at the bottom of your screen. This will take you to the Set Up Account page (see Figure 6.10).

Set Up Account

If you already use any other Google services, you may use the existing e-mail address and password you use for those services;

Figure 6.9 Review Your Selections Page
Source: Screenshots © Google Inc. and are used with permission.

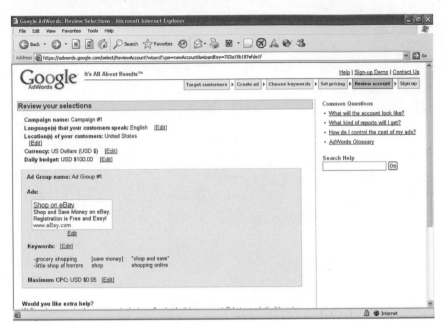

otherwise, you must select "I do *not* use these other services" and enter the e-mail address you would like to use for your AdWords account. Then choose a password, entering it twice in the fields provided before typing the characters from the distorted image in the box below it. Once you have done all this, click the Create Account button at the bottom of the screen to be taken to the "Sign-up complete" page (see Figure 6.11).

Sign-Up Complete

Once your sign-up is complete, Google will send an e-mail to the address you provided, asking you to verify your account and submit your billing information. Once you complete these steps, your ad or ads will begin showing. After verification, you can sign in to AdWords using this e-mail address plus the password

Figure 6.10 Set Up Account Page
Source: Screenshots © Google Inc. and are used with permission.

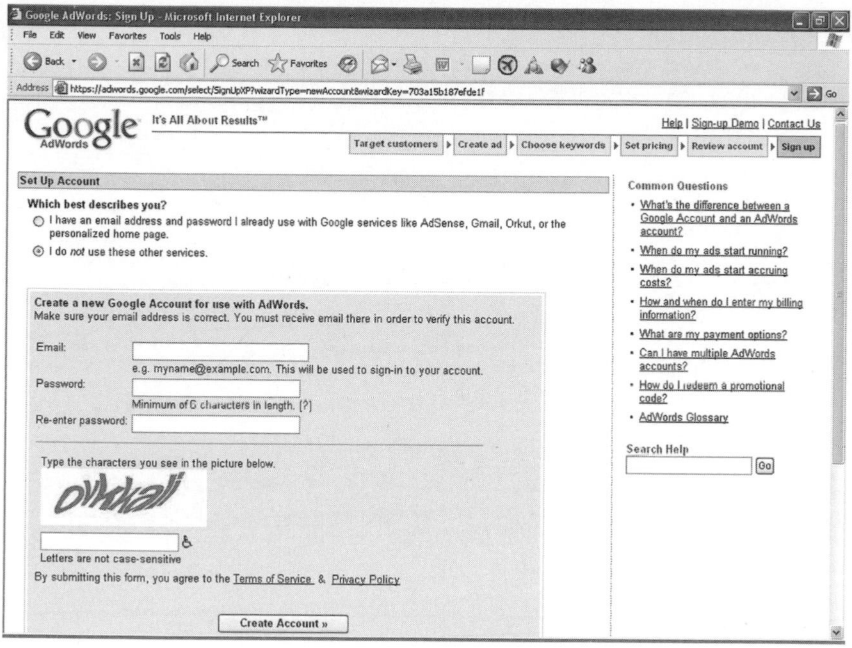

you specified earlier. Once you log back on, you will want to rename your campaign after the affiliate program it promotes. Then click on the campaign name to display the ad groups within it. The ad group you created should be renamed after the product or broad topic it advertises.

The AdWords interface is simple and intuitive, and now that you have gone through all the steps necessary to create your first campaign and ad group, you should have no problem creating additional ones. When you create additional ad groups for the same affiliate program, be sure to create them in the same campaign. When you begin promoting a new affiliate program, create a new campaign for it, and create all the different ad groups for that affiliate program within the new campaign.

Figure 6.11 Sign-Up Complete Page
Source: Screenshots © Google Inc. and are used with permission.

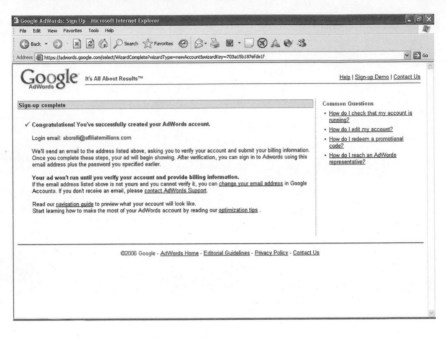

JOIN MSN ADCENTER AND CREATE A CAMPAIGN

Now I'll show you how to join MSN's adCenter program. The sign-up process for adCenter is also tied very tightly into the process for setting up your first campaign and ad group, as you will see in a moment. I will let you know when you are working on your campaign and when you are simply selecting accountwide settings. To sign up for adCenter, simply visit its home page at http://adCenter.msn.com.

AdCenter Home Page

This is the page from which you might normally log on, but you need to sign up first today, and this is what I am going to show you how to do. Look at Figure 6.12.

Figure 6.12 MSN adCenter Home Page
Source: Microsoft product screen shot reprinted with permission from Microsoft Corporation.

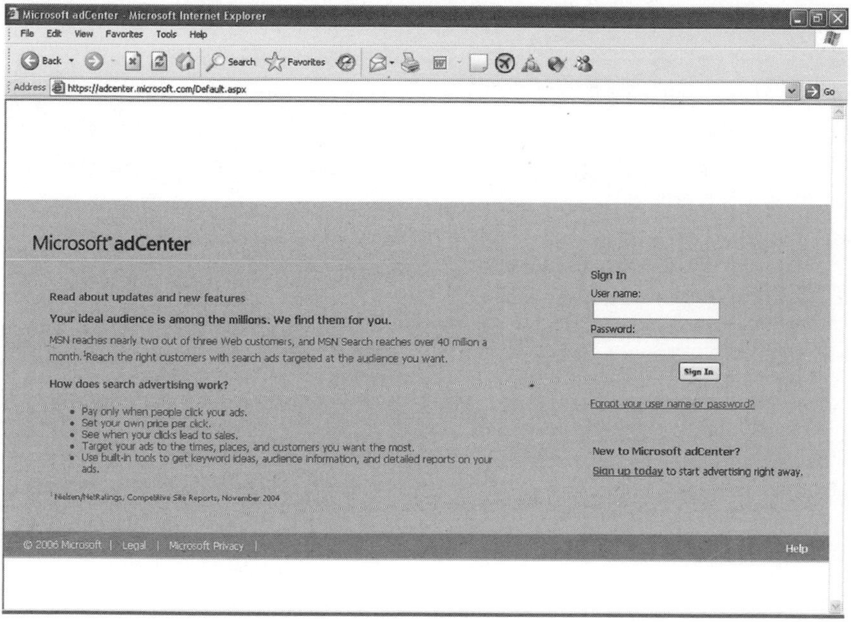

Sign Up Today. The home page of adCenter prominently features a "Sign up today" link on the lower right-hand side of the page. Go ahead and click on that link to begin, and you will immediately go to the first page of the Microsoft adCenter Account Signup process (see Figure 6.13).

Account Signup

The Account Signup page consists of three sections: contact information, communication preferences, and creating a user name and password.

Contact Information. Enter your personal and business information. Since adCenter does not, at the time of this writing, include affiliate marketing in its industry list, select Other as your industry.

Figure 6.13 Contact Information Section of the Microsoft adCenter Account Signup
Source: Microsoft product screen shot reprinted with permission from Microsoft Corporation.

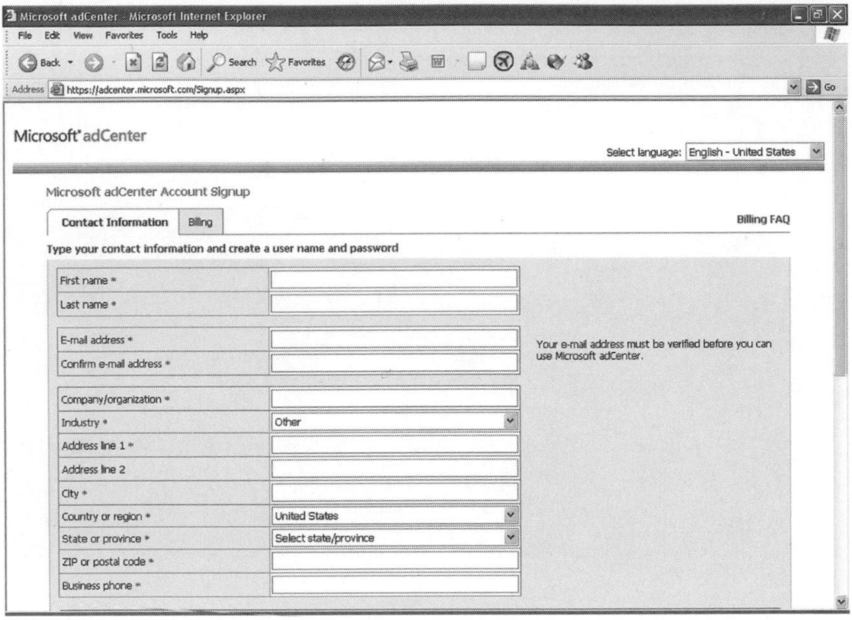

Communication Preferences. Indicate whether or not you would like to receive Microsoft adCenter member communications and, if so, how you would prefer to be contacted.

Create a User Name and Password. Enter your desired user name and password. Choose a secret question and then enter the secret answer in the field below it.

When you are finished, click Next to continue on to the Billing page of the Microsoft adCenter Account Signup.

Billing

The Billing page consists of three more sections: billing information, a promotional code box, and the terms and conditions (see Figure 6.14).

Figure 6.14 Billing Section of the Microsoft adCenter Account Signup
Source: Microsoft product screen shot reprinted with permission from Microsoft Corporation.

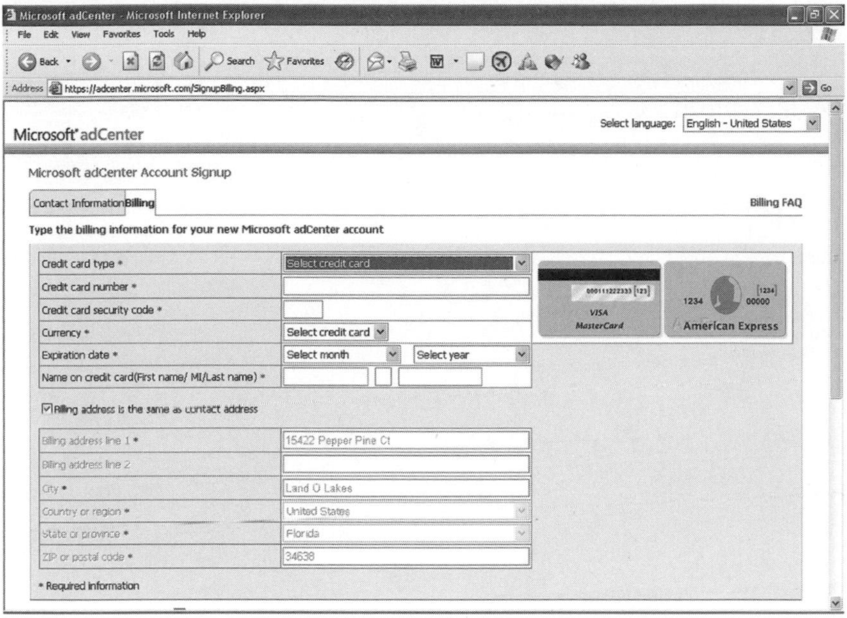

Type in Billing Information for Your New Microsoft adCenter Account. Simply enter in your billing information. You will need a credit card to participate in MSN adCenter.

Promotional Code. Enter in any promotional codes you might have. You might sometimes find promotional codes on my web site at www.AffiliateMillions.com/promotionalcodes.

Microsoft adCenter Terms of Use and Conditions. Read and accept the Microsoft adCenter Terms of Use and Conditions. Then authorize Microsoft to charge your card a $5 account sign-up fee.

When you are finished, click Submit to continue to the Signup Complete page.

Signup Complete

Click on the "Sign in and get started" link (Figure 6.15) and you will be taken to the Welcome to Microsoft adCenter page (Figure 6.16), where you can click on the "Get started now . . ." button to begin building your campaigns.

Get Started Now

Here is where you really start building your first campaign on MSN's adCenter.

Select a Campaign. Click the Create Campaign button to start creating your first adCenter campaign (see Figure 6.17). This will take you to the Settings page.

Figure 6.15   Signup Complete Page
Source: Microsoft product screen shot reprinted with permission from Microsoft Corporation.

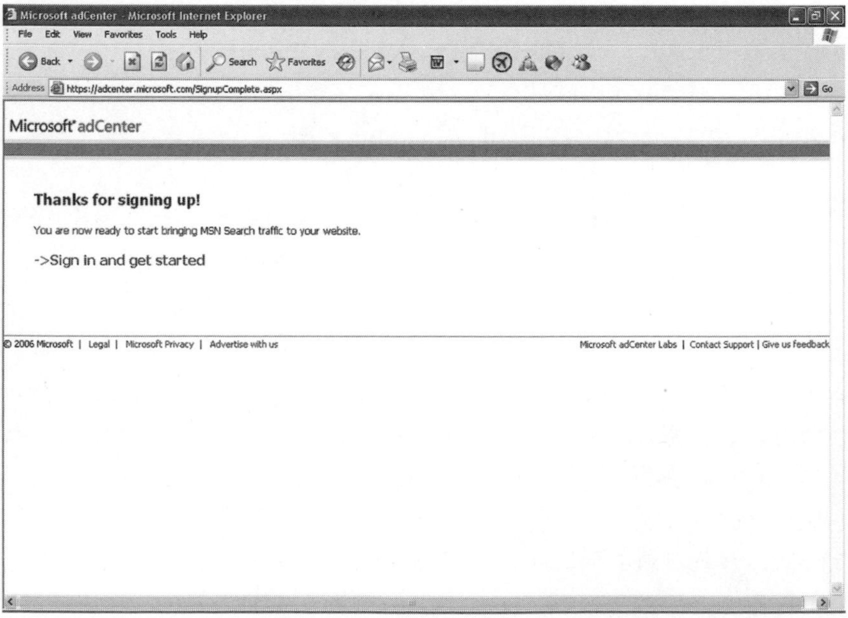

Figure 6.16 Welcome to Microsoft adCenter Page
Source: Microsoft product screen shot reprinted with permission from Microsoft Corporation.

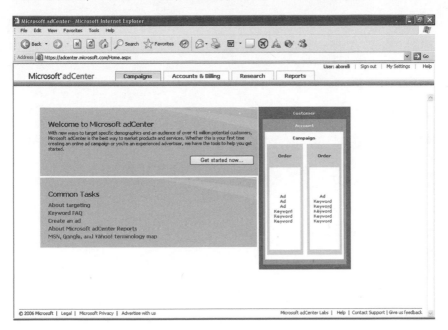

Settings

The Settings page consists of two sections: campaign and order details and targeting (see Figure 6.18).

Campaign and Order Details. The first section of the Settings page consists of "Campaign and order details." Here you will select New Campaign from the Campaign drop-down menu and enter the new campaign's name in the Name field. In this example, I am creating a campaign for Amazon, which would eventually hold all my ad groups for Amazon promotions. You will also select your time zone and name your first ad group using the Order name field (an *order* is adCenter's name for ad groups). Then select an end date, or most often, select no end date.

When you finish this section, scroll down to Targeting.

Figure 6.17 Select a Campaign Page
Source: Microsoft product screen shot reprinted with permission from Microsoft Corporation.

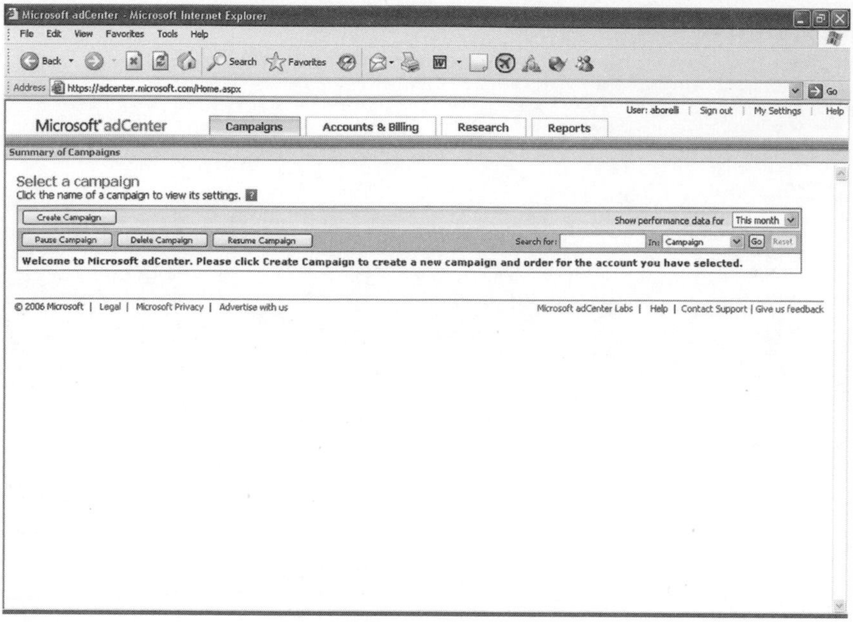

Targeting. First, you would provide the target location of your customers (see Figure 6.19). Most often you will probably choose Select countries/regions. The select your country or region from the available list that will appear, and click the Add button to place that country or region in the selected box. Then choose All days of the week and All times of the day (you can experiment with these settings much later in your career, but I do not recommend changing them for most affiliate programs).

When you are finished filling in the Settings page, click Continue to go to the Ads page.

Create Ads

The Create Ads page is where we build and save our ads. There are four components to these ads, as you can see in Figure 6.20.

Figure 6.18 Settings Page
Source: Microsoft product screen shot reprinted with permission from Microsoft Corporation.

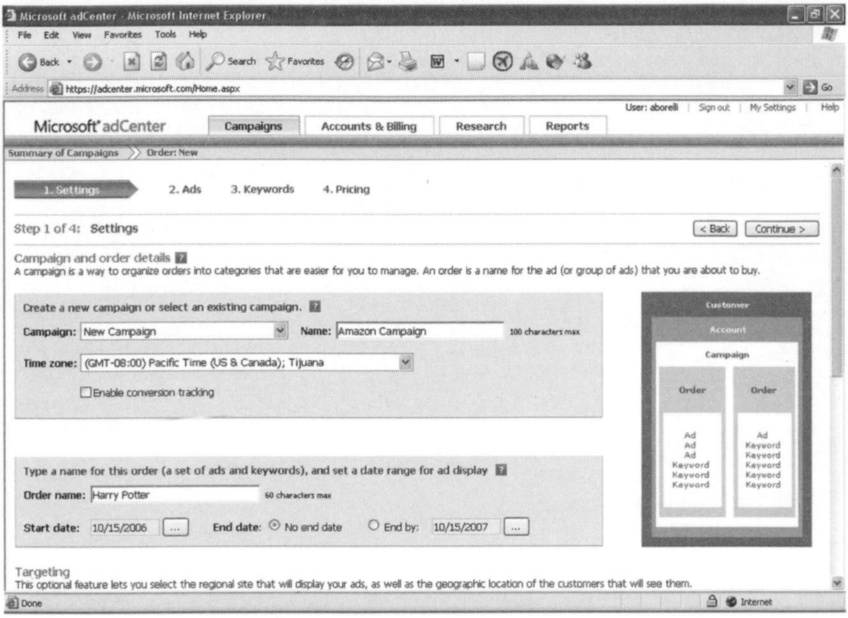

Ad Title. The ad title may be up to 25 characters long and should appropriately represent what you believe the searcher is looking for, based on the keywords you plan to bid on. This ad is narrowly focused (though not as narrowly focused as an ad for a specific Harry Potter book or movie would be), and I will probably be bidding on keywords like "Harry Potter," "Harry Potter Books," or "Harry Potter Movies." MSN also offers a keyword insertion tool (click on Dynamic Text beneath the line of the ad you are working on) to customize any part of my ad to match the user's search terms. This keyword insertion tool is a simpler version of the one we already discussed, and it works similarly.

Ad Text. As we saw before, I usually expand on the ad title with a reason or reasons for users to go to the site I promote. In the example in Figure 6.20, I have typed, "Great Deals on Harry

Figure 6.19 Targeting Section of the Settings Page
Source: Microsoft product screen shot reprinted with permission from Microsoft Corporation.

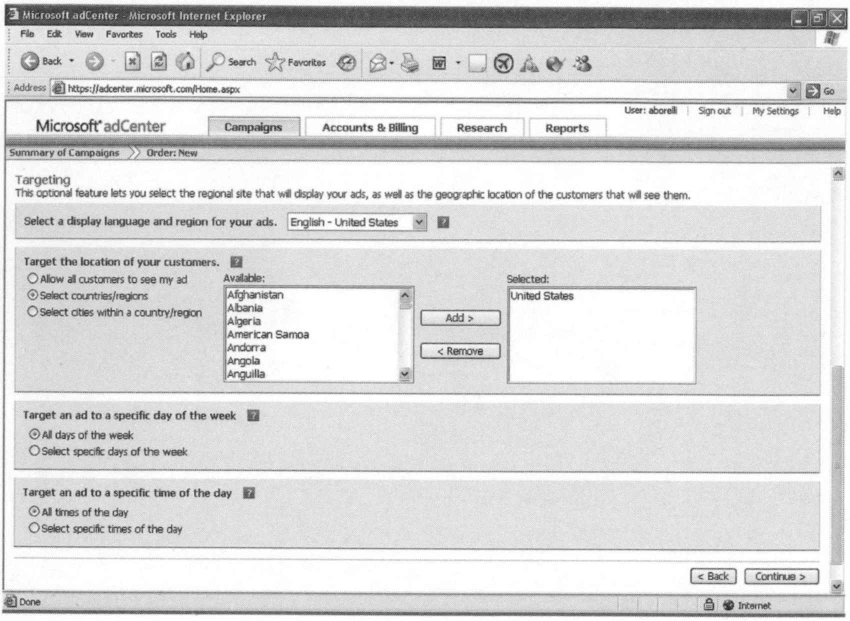

Potter Books and Movies. Free Shipping over $25!" My goal here is first to suggest that by going to Amazon instead of clicking on some other site's ad, the user will get a great deal. If Amazon also happens to be running a promotion for free shipping on orders of $25 or more, I include this in the ad as well, though now I must be sure to delete or edit this particular ad when the promotion is finished.

Display URL. This is the URL that your ad will display. It does not have to match the Destination URL, but they both must point—eventually—to the same top-level domain.

Destination URL. This is the actual URL you want customers to go to when they click on your ad, and it is here that you will enter

Figure 6.20 Ads Page
Source: Microsoft product screen shot reprinted with permission from Microsoft Corporation.

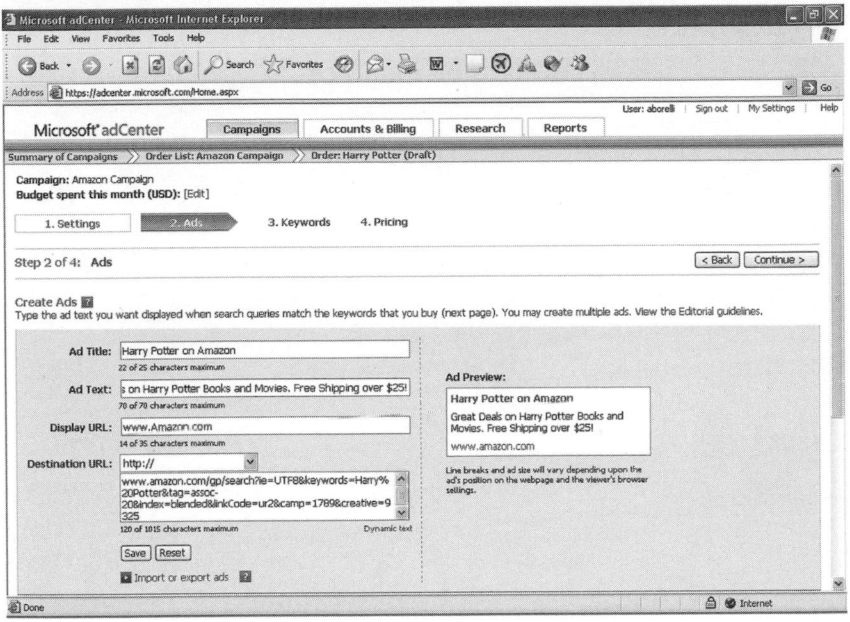

the tracking code you generated in Chapter 5 when you signed up for Amazon. Be sure to use the code you generated, *not* the example in this book, if you want to receive your commissions.

Once you have finished filling in the four elements of your ad, click Save to save your ad. You may view your saved ads by scrolling down the page a bit farther. After saving your first ad, you may create and save others, or click Continue to continue to go on to the Keywords page (Figure 6.21). Be aware that adCenter will quickly review your ad and may reject any portion of it that violates the site's editorial guidelines. Microsoft always provides clear explanations for these rejections, and you will not have any problem understanding what you've done and how to fix it if such a rejection occurs. Be aware that you can also apply for an exception if you think that adCenter's policy was not correctly

Figure 6.21 Keywords Page
Source: Microsoft product screen shot reprinted with permission from Microsoft Corporation.

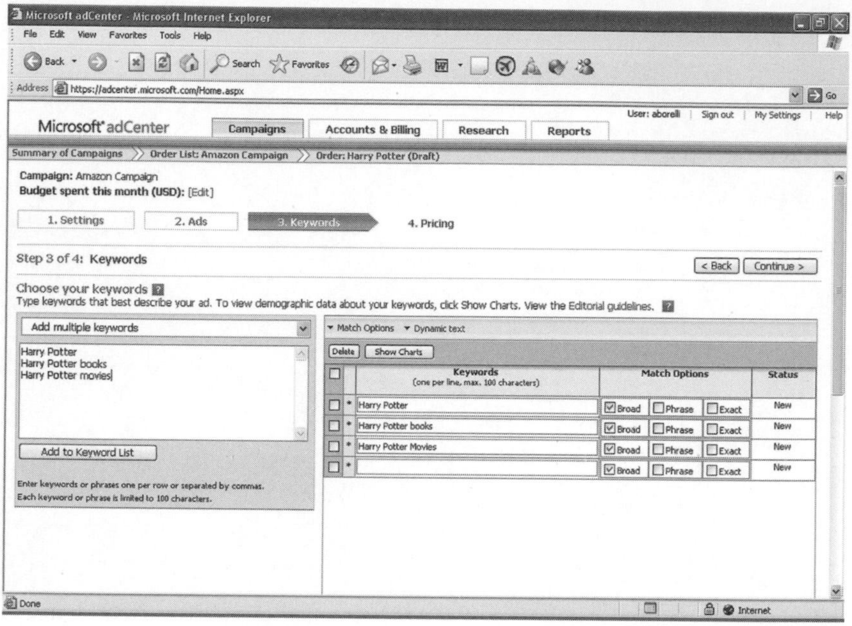

applied in any particular case, and an MSN adCenter representative will review your ad manually.

Choose Your Keywords

Here you will select your keywords. By the way, I will not be using any actual keywords that have worked well for me as examples (although these may have worked well for others, too). As I mentioned before, a few thousand people all bidding on the same keywords and running the same ads would be a surefire way to ruin my business, so you will have to find good keywords on your own.

Choose "Add multiple keywords" (or choose "Add multiple excluded keywords" for negative matching) and click on the Ad to Keyword List button to add these keywords to your list on the right (see Figure 6.21). To view and select matching options, you must click on the Match Options drop-down at the top of the list.

When you are finished entering your keywords, click Continue to go to the Pricing page.

Pricing

The Pricing page is where I start bidding on the keywords in my ad group, setting my campaign's budget, and using adCenter's traffic estimator (see Figure 6.22).

Set Bid Amounts, and Set or Modify the Monthly Budget. First, set the amount you are bidding per click for all the keywords in your ad group. I have entered my maximum base bid at 10 cents,

Figure 6.22 Pricing Page
Source: Microsoft product screen shot reprinted with permission from Microsoft Corporation.

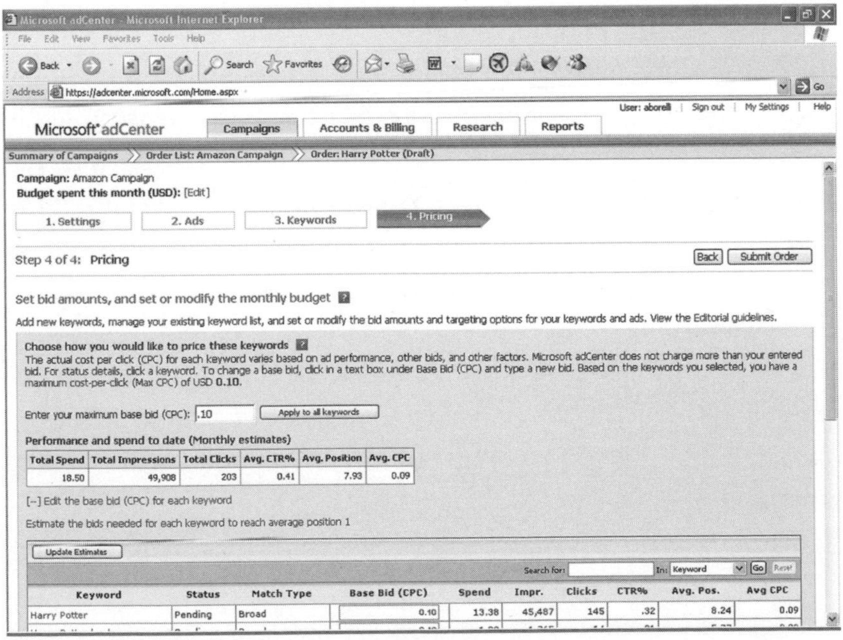

which in my experience is a good starting point for an Amazon promotion of this type. You might need to raise or lower this bid when you see what the return is, but this will do nicely to start. Click on the "Apply to all keywords" button (Figure 6.22), and adCenter's traffic estimator will do its best to predict the results. Please remember that these traffic estimators are based on the performance of existing ads, and cannot really predict how well your new ad will perform.

You will then scroll down the page. You will see an advanced option called "Set incremental pricing for targeting." However, "Do not use incremental pricing" is selected by default, and you should leave it that way. The incremental pricing feature may be a useful tool for some companies, but I have made my millions without these types of advanced options, and I suspect they can do much more harm than good in the hands of a beginner.

Just beneath this option, near the bottom of the page, is the "Set and manage campaign monthly spend" section. Here you would enter your monthly budget—$3,000 works out to roughly $100 a day—and select "Divide budget across the month" to try to keep your daily limit as close to the $100 average as possible. Remember, though, that adCenter will guarantee only that the monthly budget will not be exceeded *on average* by the end of the month. The amount you choose is dependent entirely on how much working capital you are willing to risk and your overall comfort level.

Submit Order

Once you are finished, click on Submit Order. Your order will be submitted and you will advance to the "Thank you" page (see Figure 6.23).

Now you have completed your first campaign on adCenter. Your ads will begin running as soon as they successfully complete

Figure 6.23 Thank You Page
Source: Microsoft product screen shot reprinted with permission from Microsoft Corporation.

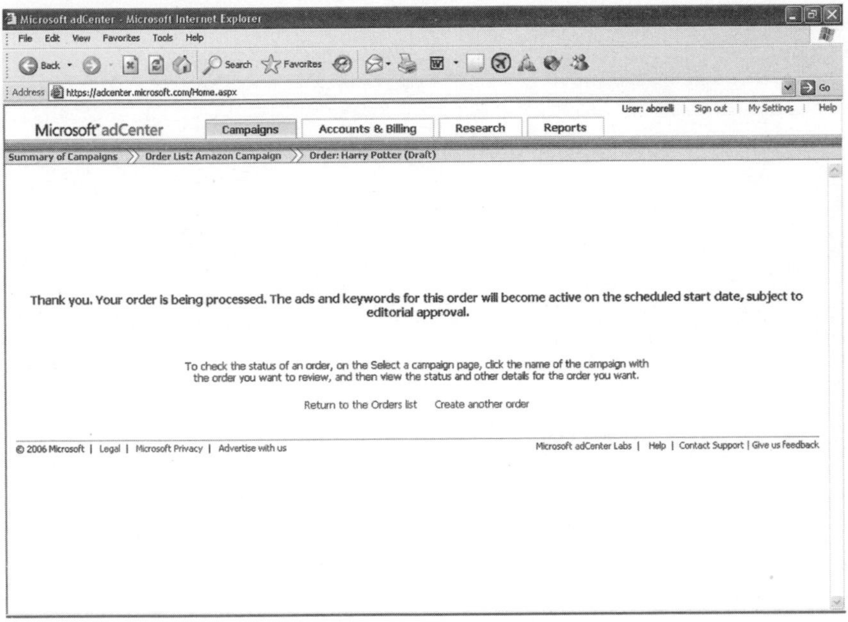

an editorial process. This differs from the AdWords program, which begins running your ad immediately, even before it is reviewed. The process can take from a few hours to a few days, so watch closely to see whether your campaign ads and keywords are approved.

In the next chapter, you'll learn how to use the reporting features of affiliate networks and search engines together the data needed to evaluate your campaigns. This information will be especially useful in Chapter 9, when you will begin performance-tuning your campaigns.

Chapter 7

Reporting

The purpose of this chapter is to show you how to determine just how much you are spending on each ad group or campaign and how much you are earning back in commission and to calculate whether or not you are turning a profit. You do this simply by adding up your earnings for a particular period of time—a day, a week, a month—then subtracting the cost of your advertising campaign for the same period of time. The remainder is your profit or loss. The information you will cull from these reports will be even more useful, however, when you reach Chapter 9 and begin performance monitoring and tuning.

AFFILIATE REPORTING

Within a day or two of starting your first campaigns, you might begin to receive reporting data from affiliate networks—although until a campaign has run for the full referral period this data is not yet fully relevant and should not be used to make any major adjustments, unless it is clear that you are spending far more than you are getting back in return. In that case, you should pause the ad group or campaign in question and wait until the end of the referral period to see whether late commissions can make up for the shortfall. The referral period, by the way, is the number of days after the original user's click for which the affiliate program will still pay commissions on the user's actions. Until this period is complete, you cannot be 100 percent sure of your actual earnings.

In order to see how much you have earned from an affiliate program in a given period of time, you must run a report on that program from within the affiliate network interface to which the affiliate program belongs. In this example, I use the Commission Junction interface to see how much my Monster.com campaign earned in the month of October 2005.

Commission Junction Reporting

First, you must log on to the CJ Account Manager using the e-mail address and password you used when you set up your account. Next, click on the Run Reports link near the top of the page (see Figure 7.1). *(Disclaimer: The dollar amounts shown are examples of a publisher's account and do not represent all Commission Junction clients.)*

On the Transaction Reports page, click on the Report Options link to expand the Transaction Reports page to include customizable report options (see Figure 7.2).

Select Report Type. On this section of the page, select Commission Detail from the Select Report Type drop-down menu, then select the affiliate program name from the drop-down menu just below it. I have selected Monster.com, as it is a campaign that had been profitable for me for a long time, even though eventually my success with other campaigns meant that maintaining this campaign was no longer worth the effort compared to the larger returns I was garnering with other programs.

Figure 7.1 Transaction Reports Page *(Disclaimer: The dollar amounts shown are examples of a publisher's account and do not represent all Commission Junction clients.)*
Source: Commission Junction

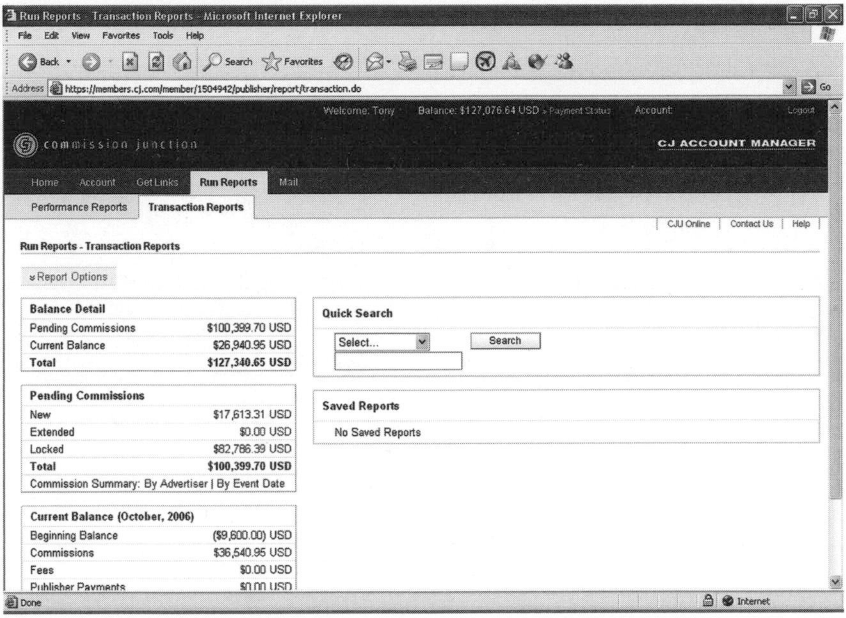

Figure 7.2 Expanded Transaction Reports Page
Source: Commission Junction

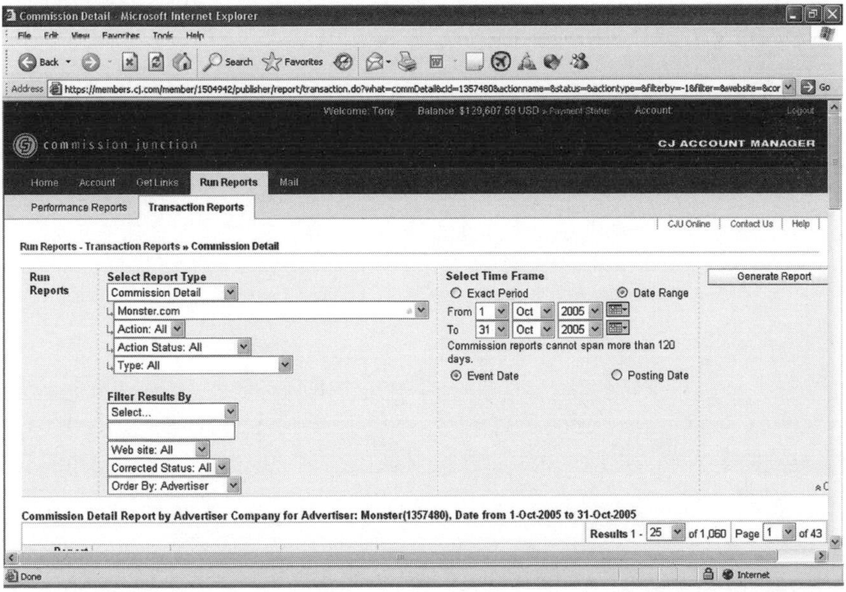

Select Time Frame. Here you will choose Date Range and enter the beginning and end dates of the period you wish to receive your report on. In Figure 7.2, you'll see that I have selected the month of October 2005. You may leave the next selection on its default choice, Event Date, and click on the Generate Report button. The results are demonstrated in Figure 7.3.

Report Totals. For this simple exercise, you may simply note that the total above the column labeled "Commission (USD)" in Figure 7.3 is $842.50. Subtract from this amount the $1.00 total you see displayed above the "Corrected (USD)" column, as this represents the transactions reversed during the reporting period. The final total earned for October 2005 was $841.50.

Figure 7.3 Commission Detail Report
Source: Commission Junction

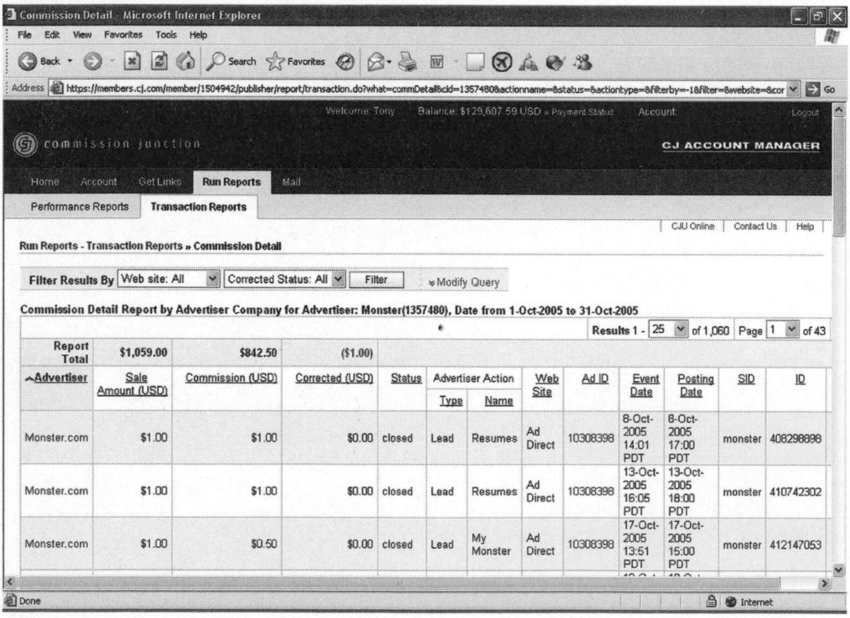

Believe it or not, this is all we really need from the affiliate side for the simple evaluation of this campaign's performance. Now, if I'd had multiple ad groups for Monster at the time, I might have needed to sort this report by SID (which is the unique variable we can add to the end of Commission Junction tracking codes to make unique tracking links for each ad group) and manually add up the results for each SID.

Let's move on to Search Reporting, then.

SEARCH REPORTING

Data from your search campaigns should be available within a matter of hours, but as I've said before, until your commission data catches up, this information is not much use. Do make sure, however, that you are spending at a reasonable rate and that you can afford to keep this campaign running until you have some commission data to work with. If you are spending more than you are comfortable with, not yet knowing your return, pause the campaign and wait until the end of the referral period for all the commission data to come in; that way you can be certain about whether or not this campaign is making more than it spends.

In order to see how much you have spent on the search marketing campaign promoting an affiliate program in a given period of time, you must run a report on the search engine or engines where you are advertising that program. In this example, I will find out how much I spent on Google to promote Monster.com in the month of October 2005.

Google AdWords Reporting

First, you must log on to the AdWords interface using the e-mail address and password you used when you set up your Google account. Once you are logged on, you should click on the Campaign in question to display the ad group, or groups, used to promote the campaign (see Figure 7.4). AdWords has a reporting page, but frankly, I almost never use it. It simply isn't necessary most of the time to get the information I need. The AdWords interface is designed to give me quick access to the data I need. Simply select the dates for which you want to see the numbers and click Go.

Report Totals. For this simple exercise, you may simply note that the total amount spent for my Monster campaign in October was only $359.99. This is all we need to know from Google to determine whether our campaign is a success or not.

Figure 7.4 Monster Campaign Ad Groups
Source: Screenshots © Google Inc. and are used with permission.

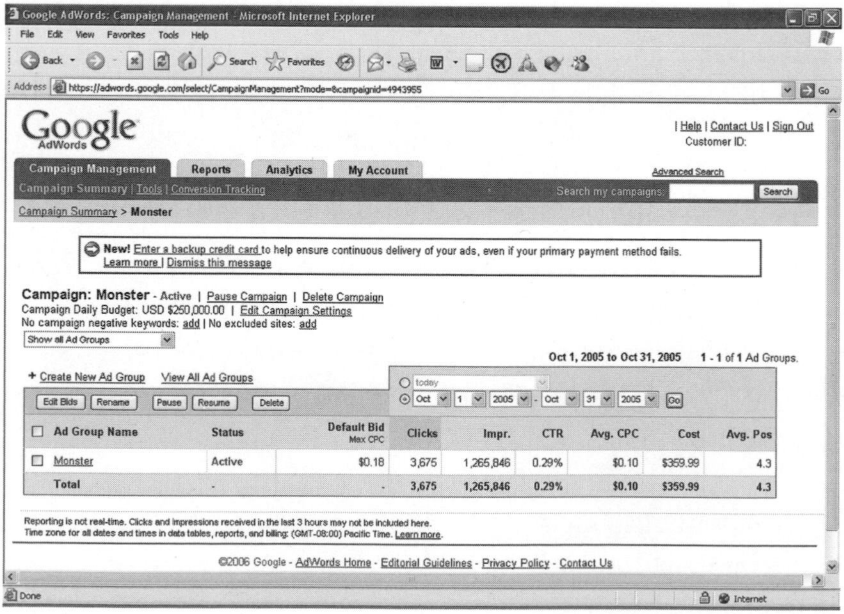

COMPARING THE RESULTS

After running two simple reports, we know that my total commissions for my Monster campaign were $841.50 and that I spent only $359.99 to generate those commissions. My profit for the month is a cool $481.51, more than double my money. You can see how building just a small number of campaigns that reach this modest level of success can help you reach financial independence, and this is only one of my most modest successes, believe me.

In Chapter 9, you'll learn how to compute this return on a per-click basis and use that figure to monitor and fine-tune your campaigns. By the way, my per-click return (net profit) in this case was almost 13 cents per click—based on the 3,675 total clicks it took to generate this profit of $481.51. So you see, everything you need to evaluate the profitability of your campaigns can be found in these simple reports.

Chapter 8

Affiliate Advertising for Web Pages

I know what you're thinking: This is a book about search marketing and affiliate advertising, not web site design. It's all about generating revenue by placing affiliate program ads on Google and other search and content networks. By publishing on search networks, you don't *have* to create a Web page. Why include a chapter about Web pages in this book? Well, the truth is, even though I have made my millions without a web site and even though I believe this is the easiest and most efficient path to success as an affiliate advertiser, many others have made and continue to make small fortunes in affiliate advertising using web sites of their own to promote affiliate programs. This chapter is not a tutorial on HTML and how to actually create Web pages, however. It is meant only to educate you on how best to incorporate affiliate advertisements into either an existing web site or one you are developing.

If you have no idea how to create a web site of your own, I can offer a little assistance though. If you visit my own web site at www.AffiliateMillions.com, you will find free HTML templates for simple web site landing pages, each with its own content theme and instructions for its proper use. These templates will only small, simple edits on your own part, primarily to rate your own affiliate ads into the page.

I have attempted only a few small commercial sites in the past and have only recently met with even minor success in this area, but if this is something you think would better suit your talents, then I have some insights to offer.

WHY CREATE A WEB SITE?

There are lots of reasons to create compelling, content-rich web sites. They can promote your business, if you have one, or they can give you a place to provide news to friends and relatives. Your site could become a soapbox from which to simply spout off on one subject or another. Web pages can also be a vehicle for promoting affiliate programs, whether these programs are secondary to the site content or the primary focus of the web site (e.g., a page comparing and promoting online degree programs, all of which might happen to be degree programs for which you receive affiliate commissions).

If you can attract lots of visitors to your web site—and I'm talking about thousands of hits (i.e., visits, or page views) each day—your site can make you money, too. In the previous chapters, you learned about some of the payment systems advertisers use to reward affiliates who place ads on their web sites and refer customers to them. In the sections that follow, you'll examine some of the content you can put on your site to gain that revenue.

HOW DO I START?

The first step to making a web site successful is focusing on your goals for the site. Do some clear thinking and planning that follows these general steps:

1. Identify your goals.
2. Decide on what type of site you want. Does your site have a product or service of its own to sell, or is it a content-based site that will rely entirely on advertisements for its revenue?
3. Identify your customers and/or audience.
4. Organize your site. Create an outline or flowchart for the web site so you have a clearly defined picture of the site's construction.
5. Determine who will create and/or maintain your web site. If you possess the time and skills required, you can do all the work yourself; alternatively, you may need to hire someone else to handle the regular upkeep.
6. Determine your budget for your site. Depending on your own skill set and how much work is required, you may need to contract with a web designer. You'll also have to pay a monthly hosting fee to your hosting service, unless you already possess the skills and equipment needed to host your own site. My web site, www.AffiliateMillions .com, has tips and links to web designers and web hosting companies and a variety of service and price points.
7. Create a timetable and stick to it. Whether you are creating a site from scratch or reorganizing and promoting an older site, you should have a clear vision of what needs to be accomplished, and in what order. Setting a timetable for accomplishing each of these goals will help you push yourself to achieve your objectives.

Coming up with a set of goals focuses you on the products, services, or content you are going to present. An organized web site that is focused on a single topic or that has a single, well-defined purpose will get more repeat visits and will induce your visitors to purchase your products and services or to remain for longer periods of time examining your content.

WEB SITES THAT CAN USE AFFILIATE ADVERTISEMENTS

A variety of sites lend themselves to affiliate advertisements, and those advertisements can transform a profitless content site into a revenue-producing site, or they can add a second revenue stream to an already successful commercial site. I list just a few for you, but the possibilities are endless.

Hobbies and Interests

Plenty of web sites are devoted to a single hobby or activity that attracts a devoted audience of collectors or individuals who share your own interests. The Web is full of sites that attract people who feel strongly about something—it may be a political cause, a social issue, a favorite movie or actor, or a series of collectible objects. The moment you attract visitors with the same interest, you stand a good chance of having them visit you regularly, because the Web appeals to anyone with a passion that needs to be shared. Repeat traffic is usually free traffic, as the users now know your name and can come to your site directly. Repeat visitors help offset the costs often associated with attracting new customers, thus giving you additional opportunities to sell your products and services—and/or those of the affiliate programs you promote on your site.

Institutional Web Sites

Many web sites function as an online "front door" or welcome page to a business or large corporation. They give the president a place to communicate to employees and to the public through a "Letter from the President," "Message from the CEO," or some

similar Web page. They typically include pages that descri
background of the organization as well as its mission or sei
The site also provides a point of contact for the visitors from the
general public, who usually get a page they can fill out or an
e-mail link they can click on to send a message to someone in the
organization.

Even though you don't have a large corporation or even a
large business, your site can perform the same functions as that of
a big institution. You can have a page in which you describe yourself and your experience or the aims of your company; you can
have another page that describes your services; and you should
definitely give visitors a way to contact you through your web
site as well.

Informational Web Sites

On the Internet, information sells. If you are able to present information that people want and make it well organized and easy to
find, you'll become a widely used resource. If you are looking for
a relatively easy way to make your site a go-to location that people will want to revisit, collect a set of links to locations on the
Internet. Try to focus on some subject that you know well and
that is related to the advertisements you plan to run. If you run
affiliate ads for institutions of higher learning, for example, you
can collect a set of links that will help people take entrance exams
or fill out applications. You can gather news headlines that relate
to college prices or trends in education. Not all of the links you
gather will have affiliate programs you can join, and some of
those links may take visitors away from your web site without
giving you any click revenue. But if those links are relevant,
up-to-date, and helpful to your customers, you'll give them a reason to return to you on a regular basis, and regular visits are the
key to long-term income on the Internet.

TIP: Check out services like AllHeadlineNews (www.allheadlinenews .com/content-services/) and the Associated Press (www.apdigitalnews .com) to get news headlines you can add to your web site.

E-commerce

Many Web sites are online storefronts such as a shopping mall, a store, a service, or other merchandise the owners have to sell. Making the move from advertising other web sites' products and services to selling your own is a substantial undertaking. However, if you already own a store or sell through another venue such as an antique mall, flea market, or marketplace such as eBay, an e-commerce web site gives you another way to reach consumers and diversify your business offerings. In order to make an e-commerce site work, you need a marketable product line, clear photos and descriptions, and a way for customers to make purchases easily and securely. That last item isn't as easy as it sounds, unless you sign up with an online shopping mall or your Internet service provider gives you access to a shopping cart (a utility that lets consumers make purchases, total them up, and hold them until checkout time) and a secure server (a Web server that encrypts information such as credit card numbers to prevent unauthorized access).

TIP: Consider signing up with a service such as Yahoo! Merchant Solutions (http://smallbusiness.yahoo.com/ecommerce/index.php). Yahoo! can provide you with utilities to create a full-featured e-commerce web site with product listings and a secure payment system, and it charges low monthly fees for you to start. Another flexible and easy-to-use solution is eBay Stores (http://stores.ebay.com).

Publishing Creative Work

If you are an aspiring writer, artist, or other creative person, you can use your Web presence to promote yourself. If you just have something to say and lots of time in which to say it, you can create an online diary or blog. Fans who visit your web site regularly may occasionally decide to check out one or more of the affiliate programs you promote, giving you a chance to earn back some of the money you may be using to promote your work.

In each of these cases, the web site types just listed can be complemented by affiliate ads. As long as you develop an audience of faithful visitors, you can use your site to gain ad revenue. The next step is to discuss the options available to you as a web site owner looking to generate advertising revenue.

WHAT TYPES OF ADS CAN I PLACE?

There are—broadly speaking—two basic types of advertisements to choose from: image ads and text ads. Depending on the circumstance, either type of ad might sometimes meet your needs better than the other, but on average (and in most circumstances) I have found that text advertisements outperform image advertisements in terms of click-through rates, conversions, and overall return on investment (ROI). I found this counterintuitive at first, and I struggled for a long time to make image ads perform for me the way text ads did, but I failed at every attempt. Of course, I have had little experience outside of search marketing, and some advertising mediums such as e-mail and pop-up or pop-under ads may not be analogous to my experience, so I encourage you to experiment with both.

Image Advertisements

Image advertisements are basically those ads that use images (as opposed to just text) to attract the viewer. I'll define two basic types: The traditional banner advertisements we still see on Web pages and in pop-ups today are one type of image ad, and the newer, rich media advertisements powered by technologies like Shockwave are another type.

Banner Advertisements. Banner ads are the traditional rectangular image ads you still see all the time on the Internet, on Web pages, and in pop-ups. The classic banner measures 460 pixels wide by 60 pixels in height—but they can come in all shapes and sizes.

Banner ads have been around since the beginning of the Internet, and you still see a lot of them. Banner ads are not as effective as text ads, in most cases, and many Webmasters believe that Web surfers simply ignore them, but the fact is that advertisers still see them as cost-effective alternatives to advertising in more expensive media such as radio and television. Well-placed and highly relevant image ads can sometimes perform very well, and oftentimes they may be more aesthetically pleasing than raw text. This may be a primary concern for some sites whose ads are a secondary revenue stream and whose professional appearance must be maintained.

Rich Media Ads. These are ads that use Shockwave or other animations to capture the viewer's attention and encourage a click. Rich media ads are generally considered to be more effective than static ads. A recent article on the advertising site ClickZ titled "The Static Banner Ad: Online Media's Little Black Dress" (www.clickz.com/showPage.html?page=3548516) claimed that rich media ads have click-through rates six times as high as static ads. In the same article, the research firm Jupiter Research was quoted as saying that by 2009 all online display ads will be rich media ads.

If you're interested in publishing rich media ads yourself,

check out the examples of video and other options at EyeWonder (www.eyewonder.com/flashAds/index.cfm).

Text Advertisements

Text advertisements are, just as the name suggests, advertisements consisting solely of text. These ads often perform very well, especially when a well-written ad is run on a page highly relevant to the ad's own content—as we have seen in ads dynamically matched to search results and content pages.

Text/Image Combinations

Combining both image and text advertisements can be an effective way to get the benefits of both mediums: the high performance of a well-written text ad and the aesthetic benefit of images. Figure 8.1 shows an example of a site geared toward helping

Figure 8.1 Text and Images Used Together
Source: Great-colleges.com

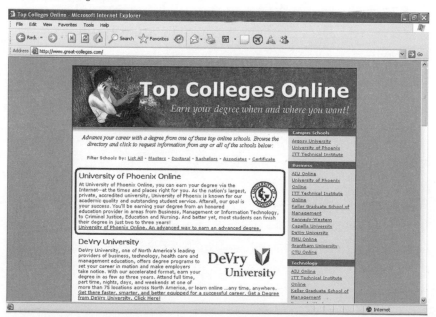

users choose and apply to college programs (colleges that offer affiliate programs pay commissions for valid applications); the site combines text and images to promote different colleges and universities.

The primary vehicle for promoting these colleges is the text: names and descriptions of the colleges themselves. The links beneath these descriptions encourage the user to visit the site now. And the long list of otherwise dry-looking text ads is broken up by the inclusion of school logos, greatly enhancing the aesthetics of the site.

WHERE CAN I GET THESE ADVERTISEMENTS?

Usually, you won't have any problem finding ads once you have joined some affiliate networks (I won't cover this process a second time here), and the process for procuring the code to place on your site is similar to the process discussed earlier, except that, unlike in search marketing—where you need only that portion of the code between the quotes in the <href> section of the code—you will need the entire code provided in order to affiliate ads on your own web site.

If your site is very unique, or if you just don't feel like poring over affiliate programs searching for the best fits for your own site, there is one option you should consider. Why not let an expert in contextual advertising, like Google, dynamically provide your site with relevant ads?

Adding Content-Focused Ads to Your Site

Programs like Google's AdSense are ideal if you want to take advantage of content-focused advertising and you run a web site that focuses on one subject in particular and draws a steady stream of visitors. The only thing you need in advance is content—content that can be tied to advertisements for products or services. If you would like to try content-focused ads, I recommend you start with AdSense. Here's how:

1. Go to the AdSense home page (www.google.com/adsense) and click on the Click Here to Apply button.
2. Fill out the form presented on the web site Information page, providing the URL of your web site and a description of its content. You need to have a web site set up before you sign up for an AdSense account; the entire program is based on advertising through a web site. Your site doesn't have to be oriented solely to your business, however; it can be a blog, a hobby site, or another site as well. The important thing is that you need to have a URL and a focus for your content on the site.

NOTE: As part of the application form, you are asked to check whether you want *AdSense for Content* or *AdSense for Search*—or both options. AdSense for Content causes the content-based ads to appear on your page. AdSense for Search causes a Google search box to appear on your page so people can search the Web directly from your site without having to go to Google. On the positive side, you gain some revenue if someone performs a qualifying action. (Some advertisers pay simply to have their ads appear; others pay for clicks; still others pay only if a purchase or registration results from the search.)

When you have finished filling out the form, click Submit Information and follow the subsequent instructions to become a member of AdSense. You will need to place some Google code on your web site, but AdSense will provide you with clear instructions on how to do this.

TIP: If you want to place an ad on your site and you host a blog, go to a site that functions as a banner ad network, such as Blogads (www .blogads.com). Blogads specializes in placing static banner ads on blog pages, and it takes care to match the content of the ad with the content of the blog.

Now that we have discussed the types of ads you might run, as well as where and how to get them, we should begin considering where on your Web pages to put them. In the next section, we discuss optimizing your ad placement on your Web pages.

WHERE AND WHEN SHOULD I PLACE THESE ADS?

When it comes to Web-based advertising, whether you are using text, images, or a combination of both, the key is to make the ads relate to the subject of the Web page on which they appear in a way that's relevant to the person viewing the page. Another important consideration, however, is the site's primary revenue stream. If it isn't affiliate advertising, then the site probably shouldn't let affiliate advertisements take customers away from the site before closing on a sale.

Where Should I Place Ads?

Where your ad appears on a site counts almost as much as what you say in the ad. Ads can appear anywhere on the page, at the top, bottom, sides or in the center, but choosing the right time and place for an affiliate ad depends a lot on what type of site you are running. The first important distinction to make is between *sales sites* and *content sites*.

Sales Web Sites. Your advertisements should be carefully placed so as not to draw the visitors away from your site before you have a chance to sell them your products or services. Running ads on or after an order confirmation page, for instance, gives a web site a chance to generate a little extra income without taking customers away before they have a chance to make a purchase from you. Other informational pages on the site, such as order-tracking pages, also offer you a chance to promote an affiliate program without distracting the customer from making a purchase.

Content Web Sites. You have a little more flexibility in placing your ads on a content web site, as advertisements likely represent the main source of revenue. Your main concern, in this case, is not to go overboard. Content is your hook for bringing these customers back, so ads should not crowd out the stories, discussion threads, product comparisons, and so on that make up the content focus of your web site.

Ideally, you want to run ads for products that are in some way related to your own product or services. If your web site was a wine-of-the-month club, for instance, then after selling customers a subscription, you might suggest a book on wines or wineries that they can find at Amazon.com. You wouldn't suggest the book on your site's main page, because that might draw customers away from your site before you sell them a subscription, which you presumably would make much more money on (possibly year after year if they are satisfied).

In some cases—product comparisons are a good example—you may be able to present your advertisements themselves as content. Say, for example, you run a product comparison web site and compare the price of the latest Harry Potter novel on Amazon, Barnes & Noble, and Half.com; there is no reason that all three price quotes cannot not use affiliate program links to take them to the item in question. Your customers get the price comparison they are looking for and you get the commission when they purchase the product, no matter which site they decide to go with.

AFFILIATE ADS AS YOUR PRIMARY WEB SITE REVENUE

Assuming you don't already have your own web site and that you are considering starting one as a vehicle for generating affiliate advertising revenue, we should spend some time discussing how to set up the kind of content web site that might accomplish that goal. It's difficult, though, to create a web site that generates a steady stream of revenue *only* from affiliate advertising. The problem is twofold:

1. *Ads drive visitors away.* By their very nature, online ads always take potential customers away from your web site. You want visitors to click on the ad, but in doing so, they'll go to the advertiser's landing page, leaving yours behind.
2. *Most of the time you won't make money.* Along with driving visitors away, you have to get used to the fact that you won't make any money most of the time when they go away. Unless you are paid by the click (AdSense and some affiliate programs still do this), only a small proportion of the clicks you generate will lead to a sale or action for which you will earn a commission.

You have two options for trying to overcome these disadvantages, and they are described in the sections that follow.

Encouraging Repeat Visitors

Repeat business is what really makes online businesses successful. The way to give visitors a reason to keep coming back to your site is to offer dynamic content that changes on a regular basis. You have to pay for the first click when visitors see your ad on a search results page and visit your web site the first time. But after that, they'll remember your site's URL and type it in regularly to view the content again and again. And these regular visits won't cost you a thing.

A good example is the Microsoft Network (MSN) web site (www.msn.com), shown in Figure 8.2. This site provides free up-to-the-hour news, stock quotes, weather, horoscopes, search functions, and more. Many people (such as myself) visit the site several times a day.

They only had to pay for me once, when I clicked on one of their ads. Ever since, MSN has had my traffic for free. Whatever MSN paid for my first visit, they probably didn't recoup right away, but over the years I have returned to this site thousands of times, occasionally clicking on its advertisements and buying products and services, and I am sure MSN has recouped its investment in me by now.

Figure 8.2 Example of a Site Using Dynamic Content to Encourage Repeat Visits
Source: Microsoft product screen shot reprinted with permission from Microsoft Corporation.

Content is not necessarily as hard to provide as you might think. I maintain a news-oriented page that has up-to-the-minute news all day and all night without any input from me. The news is provided free by Interest!Alert (http://interestalert.com), along with links to its site. I work a few ads into the content and try to make more than I spend advertising the site.

Generating Multiple Commissions from a Single Visitor

The other way to overcome the disadvantage of having only a few of your paid-for visitors actually clicking on affiliate ads is to induce some of those few to click on more than one of your ads and generate multiple commissions. My site at www.great-colleges.com (shown in Figure 8.3), is one example. I run ads for

Figure 8.3 Web Site with Potential to Generate Multiple Commissions per Visitor
Source: Great-colleges.com

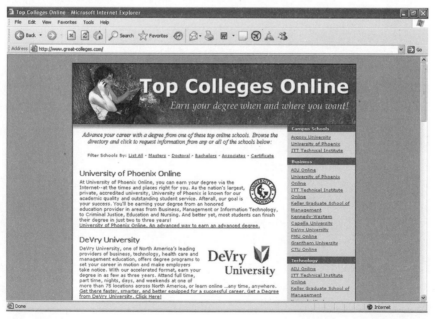

this site on Google and Yahoo! based on keyword phrases such as "earn a degree online."

If I sent those clicks straight to a single advertiser, say, Phoenix University, I might convert more individual customers than I would by sending them to my own web site, but by sending them to my web site first, I may be able to induce a few of those visitors to sign up not only with Phoenix University, but with one, two, or more other colleges as well.

Accordingly, the site is designed to provide users with a list of more than one college that meets their needs, and it encourages them to sign up with as many as possible. I have made this site barely profitable (with some search campaigns), but my volume is not yet very impressive. This is a difficult path to success, but some of you might display a natural talent for this that I do not possess, so don't let my very limited success in this area dissuade you from trying it yourself if you are so inclined.

DESIGNING A WEB SITE

As I mentioned earlier, I'm not running a Web design course, and I can't teach you the technical details of how to create your own web site. Similarly, I cannot in one short chapter teach you all the technical details of maintaining your site. What I can do is give you some general advice about what to keep in mind as you go through this process.

Many advertisers don't go to the trouble of creating full-fledged web sites. They create sites that consist of little more than pages full of undisguised affiliate links. When most people land on a page full of links like this, they immediately leave in search of a more content-rich site. You'll get more clicks if you make your site a useful resource by filling it with content that people actually want and need. To make your web site one that people will want to use, and perhaps revisit, follow the rules presented in the sections that follow.

Have Something to Offer

You can quickly tell the difference between useless pages that are filled with nothing but ads and sites that are filled with useful information. Your potential clickers can do the same. Ask yourself: "How often would I bother to use a page like that?" You're much better off spending the extra time and energy it takes to add value to your Web page by actually providing a useful service or helpful content. If your site promotes Internet gaming, don't just list a bunch of casinos. Try categorizing them and allowing comparisons by different measurements. Who has the highest initial-deposit matching program? Who offers the most favorable odds? Which casino offers the most games? What games does each offer? If users can search and filter the results list on your page to help them find exactly what they are looking for, you stand a much higher chance of winning their repeat business.

By offering not just a list, but tools with which to evaluate the sites on your list, your Web page will pique people's interest rather than turning them away.

Try to Make Your Content Unique

Previous sections have addressed the need for content that will hold visitors' interest and keep them returning to your site on a regular basis. You can add news headlines, weather, financial data, or other up-to-the-minute information. But the truth is that Web surfers can find that kind of content any number of places online. What can you publish on your web site that is unique, that no one else can duplicate? Your own personal news and views, for

one thing. Bloggers like Andrew Sullivan (www.andrewsullivan
.com) have made a good living, in part, by publishing their own
views about society and politics through blogs.

Even if you don't want to create your own blog, you can use
your Web page to talk about something that interests you, such as
your political views, your membership in a social group, or a
hobby in which you are passionately interested. By connecting
with others who share your interests, you'll build a stream of visitors. Those visitors will see your ads, and a certain percentage
will click on them. It might seem counterintuitive: Publishing
your opinions or reviews of computer programs or current events
might have nothing to do with your ads. Yet Web pages that are
personal can hold people's interest and, by doing so, can form a
good foundation for a page that can also be used to attract advertising revenue.

Keep Your Links Up to Date

One of the keys to turning a Web page into a moneymaker is simply avoiding the obvious pitfalls and turnoffs that will discour-
age traffic. One of the most obvious turnoffs is also one of the
most difficult to implement—keeping the links and other information on your site up-to-date. This is, frankly, one of the reasons
why I prefer search marketing to advertising on Web pages. Part
of the overhead of keeping up a Web page is the need to revisit it
on a regular basis (at least once a week, if not more) to keep time-
sensitive content fresh:

- Change the copyright date on the page or the "last up-
  dated" date, as needed.
- Make sure your hyperlinks all work and aren't broken.
- Add references to new sites or new information, as needed.

Software can help with at least one of these tasks: making sure your hyperlinks all work. If you invest in one of the high-end web site–creation packages described in the section that follows, you can have the software itself check the hyperlinks on your Web pages and report any that are broken. Microsoft's Expression Web hyperlinks report tool is shown in action in Figure 8.4.

Using software will go only so far, however. There's no substitute for revisiting your page on a regular basis, checking everything, and sometimes adding something new, even if it's only rewriting a heading or changing some text. Editing the text will also improve your search placement on Google, as described later in this chapter.

Finding the Right Software

The process of creating a web site is made user-friendly by the right software. The most popular and powerful Web page cre-

Figure 8.4 Some Web Creation Software Can Check Your Hyperlinks for You
Source: Gregholden.com

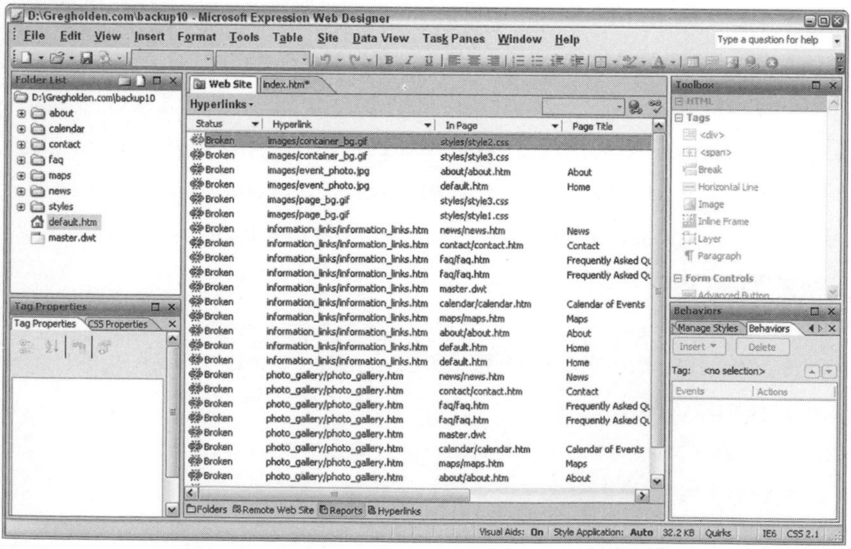

ation software is costly. But if you plan to spend a lot of time designing a site with dozens of Web pages, good software is definitely worth the expense. The first tier of powerful Web page applications include the ones listed in Table 8.1.

NOTE: When this book was being written, Microsoft's Expression Web was in beta version and not yet offered for sale. The program is intended to replace Microsoft FrontPage, which Microsoft says it will no longer support.

You don't need to spend hundreds of dollars to create a well-organized Web page or a series of Web pages. For one thing, many of the hosting services that give you access to the Internet also provide you with user-friendly utilities that allow you to assemble Web page contents by means of a Web browser. Earthlink (www.earthlink.com), one of the most popular Internet service providers, gives its users a Web-based utility for creating simple pages. America Online (www.aol.com) provides a similar utility. It can be useful, though, to sign up with a company that specializes, not in Internet access through dial-up or DSL, but in actually hosting web sites. A site like Webmasters.com (www.webmasters.com) gives customers a Web page creation utility as well as a choice of three separate shopping cart programs.

Even if you don't sign up with a Web hosting service or an Internet service provider that provides Web services to help you create your content, you can use Composer, a free Web page tool. Composer comes with both the Netscape Navigator (www.netscape.com) and Mozilla (www.mozilla.org) Web browser packages and provides you with a basic set of user-friendly tools you will need to create Web pages, including formatting controls and even a set of options for inserting and formatting tables. If you need only a Web editor that will enable you to format text,

Table 8.1 Professional Web Site Editing Software

Program	URL	Pros	Cons
Microsoft Expression Web	www.microsoft.com/products /expression/en/web_designer /default.mspx	Emphasizes CSS-based layout	Works only with Windows
Microsoft FrontPage	http://office.microsoft.com/en-us/FX010858021033.aspx	Includes powerful tools for creating forms, discussion groups, and other Web utilities	Many programs require FrontPage Server Extensions
Adobe Dreamweaver	www.adobe.com/products/ dreamweaver	Available for Macintosh and Windows; allows you to easily add interactive content such as Flash animations	Expensive
Adobe GoLive	www.adobe.com/products/golive	Makes extensive use of Cascading Style Sheets (CSS) for layout	Expensive; available for Windows only

add images, and create hyperlinks, Composer will do the job at a price you can't beat.

Securing Domain Names

As you probably know from your Web surfing, a domain name that is short and easy to remember makes it easier for you to visit a Web site—or even more likely, to revisit the site once you've found it the first time. A domain name that is short and is relevant to your web site's content gives you an additional level of credibility, too.

When it comes to choosing a domain name for a Web page that posts advertisements, it pays (literally) to take a few moments to choose a good one. Suppose someone does a search for "Top U.S. Colleges." Names that look like this don't inspire credibility:

- www.looking4goodcolleges.net
- www.top-50-colleges-list.org

Instead, visitors are more likely to click on a link that contains a shorter, clearer domain name, made up of one or two relevant words, with few (if any) hyphens and a dot-com extension rather than a dot-net or some other extension:

- www.topcolleges.com
- www.great-colleges.com

Of course, you may have difficulty finding an available domain name that meets all these criteria. Be prepared to compromise a little. To secure a domain name, you need to go to the web site of a company that functions as a domain name registrar, whose job it is to keep records of domain name ownership so the names aren't duplicated. One of the oldest and best-known domain name registrar is Network Solutions (www.networksolutions.com). But a

popular and more affordable site is GoDaddy.com (www.godaddy
.com). On either site, you do a search for the domain name you
want to see if it is available. The best-known domain is certainly
dot-com, but it's far from your only option. If an easy-to-remember
name isn't available in the dot-com domain, consider dot-net, dot-
us, dot-biz, or one of the others offered by the registrar. It's more
important to be able to create a domain name that's short and relevant to the subject of your Web page than to have one that ends in
dot-com: For example, www.goodbuys.biz is preferable to www
.i-have-lots-of-good-buys.com. You get the picture.

Analyzing Traffic to Your Web Page

Traffic refers to the number of visitors who log on to your Web
page. Analyzing this traffic is critical: When you reach a high
number of visits (e.g., 10,000) per day, you can begin to market
your page to potential advertisers and make more money from it.

Your Web hosting service or Internet service provider will
provide you with access to data from your web site's *log file*—the
reports that show how many people visited your site, where they
came from, and what other pages they visited. Pay special attention to the "referrer" pages—the pages your visitors go to immediately before they go to your web site. The pages that give you
the highest number of referrals are the ones you should put your
efforts toward when it comes to growing your business.

USING SEARCH ENGINE OPTIMIZATION TO MARKET YOUR SITE

No matter what the content of your site, you want to get exposure
for it. These days, the way to steer visitors to your web site is to
work with search and content networks, just as you already do
for your affiliate marketing. In addition to placing paid search
ads, you should also focus a large portion of your efforts on

search engine optimization (SEO). Your exposure and click traffic will increase as your site's placement within the natural search results gets closer to the top.

Search engine optimization (SEO) is the practice of adjusting your web site's organization, content, and links, and also choosing keywords that enable more people to find your site, to give your site optimal placement in search results. SEO is not an exact science, because the results depend on the formulas the search engines use to determine placement, and those formulas are often closely guarded secrets. But you can follow certain best practices that will improve your results on most search and content networks, including Google, Yahoo!, and MSN.

Submitting Your Site

Search engines have billions of different web sites in their indexes at any one time. They use automated programs that scan the main contents (e.g., the headings and the first 50 or so words on each page) and file the contents to a database. When searchers actually retrieve a set of search results, they come from the content that's been indexed in the databases, not live from the Internet.

Each of the three main search and content networks gives you a way to submit your site for inclusion in its databases. By submitting, you help speed up the process of being included by taking action rather than waiting for the automated indexing programs to find you. You also ensure that the description will read the way you want it to, because you write a description as part of the submission process. To submit your site, visit the following URLs:

- Google: www.google.com/addurl/
- Yahoo!: http://search.yahoo.com/info/submit.html
- MSN Search: http://submitit.bcentral.com/msnsubmit .htm

NOTE: Yahoo! reviews all sites that are submitted to its index, and it can take a long time to be included. If you run a commercial site, you may be required to pay a fee for inclusion.

Tweaking Your Title Bar

Simply submitting your site for inclusion in a search engine's index doesn't guarantee that you'll get good placement in search results—or even that you will be placed at all. The exact formulas search engines use for determining the rankings is a closely guarded secret, but it's generally agreed that most take into account the title bar of a Web page as well as the initial text and headings. Therefore, if you can work your most relevant keywords into your title bar, you stand a good chance of improving your search engine rankings.

The title bar of a Web page is the strip that runs across the very top of the Web browser window that is displaying that page. It displays the text that is contained within the <title> and </title> tag in the HTML code:

<head>

<title> This title text will appear in the browser's title bar </title>

</head>

Of course, your title text should also read well and should accurately represent your site if you want to attract more of the right customers.

Adding Keywords

Along with the <title> and </title> tags, the <head> section at the beginning of an HTML document can also contain META tags. These tags provide general information about the page. META tag content isn't visible in a Web browser window, but it is visible to the programs sent by search and content networks to index pages. You can add a description of your page that the search network can use when adding your page to its index. You can also add keywords that can tell the search network (in theory, at least) when to display your page in search results: If someone enters one of the keywords you have added to the META tag, your page is more likely to show up in those search results.

I say "more likely" and "in theory" because search and content networks handle keywords differently. In my experience, they do help improve your listings on Yahoo! and MSN Search. But they don't seem to make as much of a difference as far as Google is concerned.

Get Other Sites to Link to Yours

Many search engines, Google included, are very interested in how "well connected" your page is. The greater the number of links to your site from other sites, the better your chances of improving your ranking in the search results.

Keep Your Site Updated

Some search engines also monitor how often your site is updated and how much of the content actually changes. Pages that aren't updated frequently don't place well on Google and other search engines. Pages that regularly update significant portions of their content will see their search engine rankings climb as a result.

Rewriting Your Headings and Body Text

Here's one more way to improve your search ranking: Along with working your keywords into your title bar, mention as many as possible of your most relevant keywords in your Web page's main headings and in the first 50 or so words of text, while at the same time making sure you keep it readable. Some search engines may not pay much attention to the keywords in your META tags, but most do seem to consider headings and opening text.

This is by no means an exhaustive list of the steps you can take to improve your search rankings. I mention these steps because they are some of the simplest and easiest SEO steps you can take. If you wish to go further, you should consider professional assistance. A quick search on Google for "Search engine optimization" should provide you with some excellent candidates. After all, if SEOs know what they're doing, they should show up pretty high on the list.

Whatever you do, though, if you are setting up a web site of your own, don't skip the important step of optimizing your site's placement in search engine results. SEO is a popular activity on the Web, and lots of organizations and individuals are available to help you.

In the next chapter, I return to the subject of search marketing to discuss monitoring your campaign's performance, and I explain when and how to effectively tune a campaign's performance.

Part III

Managing Your
Advertising Campaign

Chapter 9

Performance Monitoring and Tuning

Nobody gets everything perfectly right the first time, and this applies to affiliate marketing as well. It's all too tempting to set up a bunch of ads and let them run on their own for weeks at a time without checking them. You need to keep an eye on your ads and monitor them carefully for a number of reasons, which I describe in the sections that follow.

WHY MONITOR PERFORMANCE?

Performance monitoring and tuning is critical to the success of any serious search marketer. The first and most obvious objective is to ensure that you are earning more than you are spending. But to be truly successful, you need to go far beyond this modest goal. You need to maximize earnings and volume while minimizing costs. Lowering bids will widen your profit margin, but it will lower your volume as well. Increasing bids will likely raise your volume, but your profit margin will shrink accordingly. Balancing these competing interests can be tricky, but there is still more to consider.

In many cases, the affiliate programs in which you enroll will include performance bonuses for higher volumes. In this case, you'll need to calculate both the cost and the benefit of generating that extra volume to determine whether to target a particular performance goal. Multiple performance tiers can complicate this task even further.

A properly tuned campaign can bring costs down *and* bring volume and earnings up. Performance monitoring and tuning can be a complicated process, but the rewards can be astronomical. I have managed several campaigns with daily earnings over $500, and my best-performing campaigns regularly earn thousands of dollars a day, so don't just settle for good enough. Make sure you maximize your earning potential for each and every campaign that you run.

PERFORMANCE MONITORING

Many search marketers make the mistake of focusing on their click-through rate (CTR) when monitoring campaigns. Although CTR is an important measurement to use when tuning your ad text and keyword selections—and you will learn more about this later—it is a mistake to rely on this single piece of data as a measurement of a campaign's overall health. The CTR of a healthy campaign can fluctuate quite a bit from day to day, without necessarily indicating that there is any problem. At the end of the day, a campaign's success is measured by one, and only one, metric . . . profit!

A more stable, and far more relevant, performance measurement is the *return per click* (RPC), and this is the primary metric I recommend for monitoring the health of your campaigns. Any change in this metric represents a change in either the *cost per click* (CPC) or *earnings per click* (EPC) of your campaign, either of which could necessitate retuning the overall campaign.

Monitoring performance is, in itself, simple enough. First, you need to calculate your return on a per-click basis, your RPC. If performance goals are in place, you will also need to calculate and project the expected return at each performance level.

You can monitor performance in one of three ways:

1.   Across an entire campaign
2.   For an ad group within a campaign
3.   For each individual keyword within an ad group

In some instances, reporting limitations— such as the inability to identify which ads your traffic comes from—will force you to monitor at the campaign level, and there will be times when tight margins will force you to monitor at the keyword level so that each individual keyword's cost and return can be monitored and tuned separately. Most often, though, you should be monitoring your campaigns at the ad group level, trusting that your ad groups are properly arranged with related keywords that will perform similarly enough to avoid the labor-intensive process of tracking each and every individual keyword's performance.

Calculating Return Per Click (RPC)

To calculate RPC, you first need to identify your cost per click (CPC) and your earnings per click (EPC).

Cost Per Click. The cost per click, or CPC, is the average cost you pay when someone clicks on one of your ads. Most search engines will calculate the average CPC for you, rounding to the nearest cent, but tight margins sometimes require that you calculate the CPC down to the first or second decimal place, so you will need to know how to calculate the CPC for yourself.

The formula for calculating the cost per click for a given day (or any other period) is as follows: Total cost divided by total clicks equals cost per click.

$$\text{Total cost} \div \text{total clicks} = \text{CPC}$$

For example, if campaign XYZ spent $200 yesterday and generated 1,054 clicks, your calculation for the cost per click would look like this:

$$\text{CPC} = \$200 \; / \; 1054 = \$0.189$$

So your CPC for the day is 0.189, or, rounding up, about 19 cents.

Earnings-Per-Click. Your earnings per click, or EPC, is your return on your pay-per-click advertising investment. This return comes to you in the form of commissions from affiliate programs. Accurately calculating your EPC can be complicated, as most affiliate programs will pay commissions on customer actions for a certain number of days, weeks, or months after the original click that brought that particular customer to their site. This is called the *referral period*. Fortunately, in most cases the lion's share of your commissions will occur on the same day on which the click occurred. That being the case, I suggest a simplified method for calculating EPC, using the commissions earned during the same day (or other period), regardless of when the original click occurred. In the beginning, this method will slightly underestimate your EPC, but once you have been operating at a steady volume for the full referral period (usually between 7 and 30 days), this method will very closely approximate the actual EPC without the accounting nightmare of trying to match up original clicks to late commissions.

Here is the simplified formula for calculating your earnings per click: Commissions earned divided by total clicks equals earnings per click.

$$\text{Commissions earned} \div \text{total clicks} = \text{EPC}$$

If campaign XYZ from our earlier example earned $253 yesterday on the 1,054 clicks it generated, the calculation would look like this:

$$\$253 \div 1054 = \$0.240$$

Your EPC in this case is 24 cents.

Return Per Click. Now that you know your CPC and your EPC, you are ready to calculate one of the most important measures of a campaign's performance, the return per click (RPC).

The formula for calculating the RPC is a simple one. Your earnings per click minus your cost per click equals your return per click.

$$\text{EPC} - \text{CPC} = \text{RPC}$$

For example, you have already calculated that EPC for campaign XYZ is 24 cents and that its CPC is 19 cents, so the formula for calculating the RPC is simple:

$$\$0.24 - \$0.19 = \$0.05$$

Your RPC is 5 cents. In other words, every click that campaign XYZ generated yesterday earned a net profit of 5 cents.

Your return per click represents your net profit (or loss) each time an ad is clicked on from the campaign or ad group you are watching. Later, during the performance-tuning section of this chapter, you will learn how to maximize your profits and determine what your ideal RPC should be. Once a campaign is successfully tuned for optimum earnings, the RPC should remain within a certain range (which is different for every campaign) during the performance period. The RPC is a composite of two metrics (CPC and EPC) that should both remain fairly stable in a healthy campaign, and a change in either metric will show up in your RPC. Monitoring the RPC for any sudden changes outside its normal range of fluctuation will help you recognize when these campaigns are running smoothly and when their performance needs tuning, which I discuss later in this chapter.

Calculating and Projecting RPC for Performance Goals

So far, calculating RPC is a simple and straightforward process, but what happens when affiliate programs introduce monthly or quarterly performance goals to their commission structure? The answer is, if you are to have useful data with which to tune an ongoing campaign within its performance period, you will now need to begin calculating and monitoring your *projected* RPC (pRPC). To calculate the pRPC, you will need to first project your costs, earnings, and clicks for the period.

For the purposes of this exercise, let us say that you are trying to project your performance for the month of June. Your performance goals are based on gross sales, and you have three full days of data to work with. As of June 3, you have spent $15 dollars on an ad campaign that generated 200 clicks to your client,

Jungle.com. The result to date from your ad's traffic at Jungle.com has been $600 in gross sales. Keep in mind that this is $600 in *gross* sales, not commissions. Your commission will be much smaller, depending on which performance tier you reach. You are looking only at gross sales right now, because this is the measurement on which your performance is judged.

Projecting Costs. To project your total costs at the end of June, you need to know only how much you have actually spent, how many days of complete data you have (in this example you have three days of data), and the length of the performance period (30 days in June).

$$\text{(Costs to date} \div \text{number of days passed)} \times \text{performance period} = \text{projected costs}$$

If you have spent $15 through June 3, then the formula looks like this:

$$(\$15 \div 3) \times 30 = \$150$$

So your projected cost for June is $150. Now we move on to projecting your earnings for the month of June.

Projecting Earnings. To calculate your projected earnings, you need to begin paying closer attention to your volume. What is volume? How you measure volume will vary from affiliate program to affiliate program. If the performance goals are tied to total sales in dollars, then you will measure, track, and project your volume in total sales. Should the client's performance goals be tied to the number of items sold, then you will measure your volume in items sold. If the performance goals are tied to new member registrations, then you will measure volume by the number of new registrations.

Next, you need to project what your total volume will be at the end of the performance period. Let us say your performance goals are tied to total monthly sales. You need to project what your volume (in this case monthly sales) will be at the end of the month, based on sales to date. The formula is as follows:

$$\text{(Volume to date} \div \text{number of days passed)} \times \text{days in the month} = \text{projected volume}$$

If you have generated $600 in gross sales for your client through June 3, then your projected volume calculation for June would look like this:

$$(\$600 \div 3) \times 30 = \$6,000$$

So your projected volume for June is $6,000. Now that you have projected your sales volume, you need to determine which performance tier that projected volume puts you in.

In Table 9.1, you can see that your projected volume of $6,000 puts you in the 5 percent performance tier. Now you will calculate your projected earnings by multiplying your projected volume by the projected performance tier.

Table 9.1 Example of Performance Goals

Jungle.com
Monthly Performance Tiers

Total sales:	$0 – $999.99	3%
	$1,000 – $4,999.99	4%
	$5,000 – $9,999.99	5%
	> $10,000	7%

$$\text{Projected volume} \times \text{projected performance tier}$$
$$= \text{projected earnings}$$

In this case,

$$\$6,000 \times 0.05 = \$300$$

So your projected earnings for June equal $300.

Projecting Click Volume. Projecting your click volume is more straightforward. If, as in the preceding example, you have generated 200 clicks in the first three days of June, you can calculate as follows:

$$(200 \div 3) \times 30 = 2,000$$

Thus, you can project about 2,000 clicks by the end of June.

Calculating the pRPC. With this final piece of information you are ready to calculate your pRPC by first subtracting your projected costs from your projected earnings to get your total projected return, then dividing your total projected return by your projected click volume to get your pRPC.

$$\text{Projected earnings} - \text{projected costs}$$
$$= \text{total projected return}$$

$$\text{Total projected return} \div \text{projected click volume} = \text{pRPC}$$

Let's fill in the equation with the results from your June example:

Your total projected return is: $300 − $150 = $150

Your pRPC is: $150 ÷ 2,000 = $0.075

Now you know that at your current pace, you will finish the month of June with a $150 profit (your total return) and that you are netting between 7 and 8 cents per click (your pRPC). But what do you do with this information? Is this a good pRPC? In the second part of this chapter I discuss how to maximize your projected earnings and identify an ideal pRPC. Once a campaign has been successfully tuned to optimize performance, you can expect the pRPC to remain within a certain range, and you should monitor it for any sudden changes outside its normal range of fluctuation.

When monitored daily, the RPC (or pRPC) can be an excellent indicator of your campaign's overall health and provide an early warning signal when a campaign is in need of tuning. In many cases, seasonal fluctuations in volume that can affect your overall earnings will not affect your RPC, and by relying on RPC instead of earnings, volume, or click-through rates as your primary indicator, you will spare yourself the frustration of trying to fix something that may not be broken. Your pRPC is more vulnerable to seasonal fluctuations, but when you are dealing with tiered commission structures, seasonal performance tuning is often necessary, and so the pRPC remains a valid primary indicator when deciding whether a campaign is in need of a tune-up.

PERFORMANCE TUNING

But what about a new campaign or an existing campaign that may be underperforming? When a change in your RPC alerts you that performance tuning might be necessary, the RPC is no longer your primary focus. Your goal for performance tuning is always to maximize your total return, and the trade-off between volume and margin (RPC) is the dynamic you need to be most aware of.

Consider Table 9.2. In week 3, the RPC alerted you to a potential tuning issue when it jumped from 5 to 9 cents per click. At first glance, this may have appeared to be a positive change. After all, your Munster Jobs campaign is making almost twice as much

Table 9.2 Campaign in Need of Tuning

Munster Jobs

Monitoring Worksheet for January

	Total Clicks	Total Cost	CPC	Commissions Earned	EPC	RPC	Total Return
Week 1	3,411	512.04	$0.15	695.61	$0.20	$0.05	$183.57
Week 2	3,589	521.89	$0.15	705.25	$0.20	$0.05	$183.36
Week 3	2,506	265.57	$0.11	503.49	$0.20	$0.09	$237.92
Week 4	1,257	125.06	$0.10	256.34	$0.20	$0.10	$131.28

per click, and although your click volume has dropped, your total return has actually increased significantly. Even so, the dramatic change in RPC should have alerted you to the fact that a significant change has occurred, and even if this change is positive, the campaign still needs to be tuned to maximize potential earnings in this new set of circumstances. In this example, however, the decision was made not to tune the campaign.

In week 4, the positive trend in lower CPC and higher RPC continued, but was eclipsed by the accelerated downward trend in click volume. The end result is a precipitous drop in the total return, which can be expected to continue if you do not do something.

It is very tempting at this point to ask, "What has happened? What has changed?" Perhaps the addition of an aggressive bidder has lowered your ad position, or perhaps another ad for Munster Jobs written by some other search marketer has replaced you in the paid search algorithm. Maybe a subtle change has occurred in the algorithm itself. Perhaps another campaign has widened or narrowed its focus on keywords and phrases to include your own—or to exclude something you missed. There are a number of possibilities, but I cannot stress enough that it does not matter what the cause of the change might be. The solution is the same: Refocus everything to maximize your total return in the new environment.

Looking back on some of my earlier successful campaigns, and the hurdles I overcame, I can see that I benefited enormously from my complete ignorance of what external factors might actually have been affecting my campaigns. This sounds strange, I am sure, but because I did not know or even imagine what these external factors might be, I was forced to cover all my bases.

Had I known, for instance, that my competitor's ad was now running above mine because of a higher click-through rate, I likely would have focused all my energy on retooling my ads to obtain a higher CTR. But higher CTRs do not guarantee higher RPCs (in fact, in many cases they lower them), and simply by tuning your entire campaign to run as efficiently as possible in your new environment, you can remain profitably near your original position while you wait to see whether your competition can really afford to maintain his or her own new position. A higher CTR, for instance, may mean your competition's ad is promising too much, and that person's RPC could be far lower than your own. Oftentimes, your competition will need to make changes of his or her own to stay profitable, possibly returning the environment to its original state. Patient search marketers who know how to make what they can in a new environment will often find themselves comfortably back in their original position within a matter of days.

The important thing to remember when you are performance tuning is to make certain that *everything* is tuned. You must go through each step, one at a time, taking as many hours or days as you need in between to allow your monitoring to reveal whether your changes improve your total return and then reversing the changes that do not improve your total return. Some tuning options may not be necessary or may require only a small adjustment, but make sure to check everything at least twice, and don't stop going through these tuning steps until you find you can no longer significantly improve your total return by adjusting them. I know this process sounds long and tedious—and it can be—but I firmly believe that a thorough and deliberate tuning routine can give you a big edge against the competition.

One last thing before you start actually tuning your campaigns. Always double-check your maximum daily budget first and be certain that it is still set at an amount you are willing and able to risk. Also, be aware that for some high-volume keywords on some search engines, your daily budget limitation might be reached so quickly that it is exceeded before the ad can be shut off. I have had campaigns spend several times my daily budget within an hour or two on more than just one occasion, so if you are bidding on a keyword with obvious volume potential, you need to be especially cautious.

Tuning Your Keywords

You have already covered the keyword selection process, how and when to group them into ad groups, and when to use keyword phrases, exact match, broad match, negative match, and the like. The key now is to simply revisit this same process. Can you think of any keywords you missed? Negative matches? Maybe Paramount Pictures has decided to release a movie remake of *The Munsters*, and your Munster Jobs campaign should now include some negative keywords to weed out those interested only in the upcoming movie and not in the job site you are advertising. Maybe you change some of your broad matches to phrases or exact match. Make any changes you feel might be necessary, but do not make changes without any reason just to see what happens. If you went through the original keyword selection process carefully and thoughtfully, this area will likely need the fewest changes when tuning.

Tuning Your Bids

Obviously, the higher you bid, the more often your ad will run and the higher your position will be, which will result in more clicks (budget allowing). You will also see higher costs and lower returns per click. The lower you bid, the less often your ads will run and the lower your ad position will be, but your costs will go down and your RPC will go up. So the question you should ask is, do you need higher volume or higher margin (RPC)?

In the example shown in Table 9.2, you can see that your margin is more than just fine, it has actually grown, and your problem is clearly your plummeting click volume. In this case, you would raise your maximum CPC bid, probably by at least the 5 cents per click you seem to be saving already in your actual CPC. Then you would continue to monitor your total return and continue to raise your maximum bid in increments until you find the bid that gives you the highest total return.

If your volume is fine, but your margin (RPC) is very low, then you head in the opposite direction. You would lower your maximum bid incrementally while still monitoring the total return to determine the most profitable bid.

How much you should raise or lower your bids each time is another question. I cannot provide you with an exact answer or a simple formula, but there are a couple of things to keep in mind. Certainly, you should never raise your maximum bid much higher than your earnings per click (EPC), as this could result in your campaign not just losing money per click, but also in generating more clicks (potentially a lot more clicks) and losing more money. And, if you raise or lower your bids only in tiny increments, this process could be agonizingly long. Outside of these two pieces of advice, you are left to your instincts. But be aware, the more aggressively you proceed through this process of tuning your bids, the more closely you should monitor the results.

Tuning Your Ad Text

I said it before and I say it again: Ad copy is *king*. In performance-based paid search algorithms such as Google, MSN, and (soon) Overture (i.e., Yahoo!), a good piece of ad copy can lower your costs *and* increase your volume, so be sure to invest some time in testing your successful ads against new ones. I have already discussed how to write good ad copy and things you should consider when putting an ad together, so your focus now should be on implementing what you have learned: writing multiple ads, comparing them against each other, and sorting out the great from the merely good.

First, you should never edit an existing successful ad—that is, an ad that has generated a substantial number of clicks with a positive EPC—unless you have a more successful ad already in place. I have been told by Google that ad history is a factor in its paid search algorithm, and I am sure Google is not the only one doing it. Always create a new ad, even if it will have only minor changes from the original, and run these side by side. You must be sure to run these ads long enough to get a statistically significant sample. This is not a text on business statistics, so if you are not sure what that means, just wait for two days or until you have 200 clicks, whichever comes first. Do not run more than two or three ads against each other at once. If you have half a dozen different ad ideas you want to try, run the first two against the existing ad, and whichever of the two challengers appears the weakest can be replaced with one of the ads you haven't tried. Do not replace your original ad, even if it is underperforming the new ad(s), until the more successful ad has built up a strong history.

This history does not necessarily need to include more total clicks than the old ad—in some cases you may have spent years building up the ad history for the old ad—but the new ad should generate a significant number of clicks, operate for at least one full performance period, and the all-time CTR for the new ad should be at least as high as the all-time CTR of the old one. Your primary metric for comparing these ads will be the click-through rate (CTR) of each ad during the time they run against each other, but you will also keep an eye on your total return. As discussed in Chapter 6, if your ads overpromise or fail to filter out the bad leads, then the increased traffic may not lead to increased commissions, and CPC savings might not offset the drop in EPC. But once again, the bottom line is always . . . the bottom line.

When you believe you may have created a better ad based on a higher CTR, monitor your total return for at least a few days to ensure that it does indeed go up. If the total return goes down significantly, your new ad is a lemon, and you should stick with the old one. If the total return is significantly higher, your new ad is a keeper, and you should run it beside the old ad until it has built up a similar history, at which time you will delete the old ad. If your total return is not significantly higher or lower but is instead rather flat, then you should probably still transition to the new ad, though somewhat more cautiously. Even though this new ad may not be making more money for you, your higher CTR is probably translating to higher costs for your competition, and as long as you are not losing money to accomplish this, in the long run it can only help you.

Tuning Your Budgets

Initially, you set your daily budget with the primary goal of limiting how much you are willing to lose while taking a chance on a new campaign. Once you have determined that your campaign has potential, your focus will switch to tuning.

Budget tuning is a simple enough process. Your first goal in setting a daily budget is to keep your costs in line. You want to ensure that you do not run out of money, and as your advertising bill will have to be paid several weeks before your commissions will be paid out to you, you must make sure your daily budget is set at a level that will allow about 60 days based on the cash you have on hand to pay for advertising. For example, if you have only $600 on hand, you do not want to spend much more than $10 a day, or you run the risk of having to shut off your campaign, which would allow your competition some number of days or weeks to operate in the same space without the price pressure of your presence.

Your second goal is to allow a profitable campaign to generate as much traffic and income for you as possible. Over time, as you become more and more successful, you should find you have a good deal more money with which to buy more clicks. As your bankroll grows, you should continue to raise the daily budgets of your most successful campaigns until you find they are no longer able to give you more traffic than you can afford.

Each time you improve your keyword list, raise your bids, or perfect your ad text, you must revisit your daily budget to make certain it still meets your twin goals of generating as much traffic as possible and ensuring you do not run out of cash before your next commission check arrives.

Tuning to Meet Performance Goals

By far the most complex task you will undertake in this business is to performance-tune a campaign for an affiliate program that includes performance goals or a tiered commission structure. Don't panic, it isn't rocket science, and I have an approach that should make it far simpler for you than it was for me in the beginning.

The first thing you need to be aware of is how the performance metrics we have discussed can function as simple levers that allow you to increase or decrease at will the traffic your campaigns generate. These two metrics are your keyword list and your maximum bid amount (and, of course, you must remember to adjust your budget to allow this additional traffic). By raising your bids or expanding your keyword list—either through broader matching or additional keywords—you can increase the traffic of a successful campaign pretty much at will.

Normally, you would raise these metrics only until you see your total return level off or start to drop, but with a tiered commission structure, pushing these metrics further, even as the total return dwindles, might make sense if you can increase that traffic just enough to reach the next tier, at which point, a higher rate of return for all of your sales/leads could push the total return back into positive territory, and possibly even push it above its previous peak within the lower tier.

Your plan, then, must be to raise your bids and/or expand your keyword list for a few days in order to capture enough data to determine (1) whether you can generate enough business volume to reach the next performance tier and (2) whether your total return at the new performance tier will be able to exceed your total return at the old performance tier. After capturing a few days' worth of cost and return data with your higher bids and/or expanded list of keywords and phrases, you must project (as you learned how to do earlier in this chapter) what your total return would be if you left these metrics at these higher levels for an entire performance period (usually one month or one quarter).

Let us say, for instance, that you double the maximum bids for three days for your Jungle.com campaign from earlier in this chapter. You must, after all, generate at least $4,000 more than the $6,000 you projected in June in order to reach the $10,000 tier. In those three days, you generate 350 clicks at a cost of $39. Your plan to generate more click volume by paying more per click has succeeded, but did you reach the next performance tier? Your sales for this three-day period increase to $1,050. Now you will once again project your costs and earnings using the same formulas.

(Costs to date ÷ number of days passed)
× performance period = projected costs

If you have spent $39 in three days, then your formula looks like this:

$$(\$39 \div 3) \times 30 = \$390$$

So your projected cost for the month if you maintain the higher bids is $390. Now you move on to projecting your earnings. Your formula is as follows:

(Volume to date ÷ number of days passed)
× days of the month = projected volume

If you have generated $1,050 in gross sales for Jungle.com in three days, your projected volume calculation would look like this:

$$(\$1,050 \div 3) \times 30 = \$10,500$$

So your projected volume is $10,500. It appears that your higher bids have generated enough additional volume to reach the 7 percent performance tier, but was it worth the cost? Let's calculate your projected earnings at the new performance tier and subtract your projected costs to come up with a projected total return to compare to your June figures.

Projected volume × projected performance tier
= projected earnings

In this case,

$$\$10,500 \times 0.07 = \$735$$

So your projected monthly earnings at the higher bidding level are \$735.

Finally, you will project your total return.

$$\text{Projected earnings} - \text{projected costs}$$
$$= \text{total projected return}$$

$$\$735 - \$390 = \$345$$

Your projected total return at the higher bidding level is \$345. This is considerably higher than your June projected return of only \$150, so if you began this experiment at the beginning of the month, you would leave the higher bids in place. If you began your test in the middle of the month, however, you would probably return your bids to the normal level, as you would not be able to reach the \$10,000 performance tier with only a week or two remaining. At the start of the next month, you would again implement the higher bids.

Keep in mind, as you are just barely reaching this performance tier, you need to watch this campaign very closely to be sure you do not miss your goal. If this means raising the bids a little higher in the last days or weeks of the month, then that is what you should do. If your actual sales figures come in lower than projected, say at \$9,900 for the sake of this argument, your whole formula changes. Since you did not reach the \$10,000 performance goal, you must now calculate your earnings at the 5 percent level.

$$\$9,950 \times 0.05 = \$497.50$$

So your monthly earnings if you just miss the performance goal could be just \$497.50. What is the effect on your total return?

$$\$495 - \$390 = \$105$$

So you see that if you increase your spending to reach the 7 percent performance tier and you just miss it, you could make considerably less than you would have if you had optimized the campaign for the 5 percent performance tier you actually finished in. In fact, you could do a lot worse than shown in this example and actually *lose* money on a campaign that was once profitable when optimized for the 5 percent tier. The lesson here is this: When you are shooting for a performance goal, make sure you hit it, or bail out early.

Campaigns with Multiple Ad Groups

There is one last complicating factor: performance-tuning multiple ad groups for a single campaign. You learned earlier that some campaigns would require multiple ad groups to manage multiple product lines that require dissimilar ads, keyword lists, and bid amounts. If the affiliate program promoted by the campaign has no performance tiers, then you can and should simply monitor and tune each ad group separately, ignoring the fact that they are part of the same campaign. When performance goals are introduced into the picture, however, these various ad groups are now dependent on each other. Since the performance tier will be determined by their combined performance, their individual returns will vary depending on how well all ad groups perform together. Now you will see how this affects you during the performance-tuning process.

Consider Table 9.3, based on three days of data, separately projecting monthly totals for multiple ad groups in your BuyIt .com campaign, an affiliate program with performance tiers.

At first glance at these projections, you might assume that your Toys ad group should be turned off, or at least have its bids lowered to bring costs down. After all, it is the only ad group in your BuyIt.com campaign not making a profit. A closer examination

Table 9.3 Multiple Ad Groups Supporting a Single Campaign with Performance Tiers

BuyIt.com Projection Worksheet

Monthly Performance Tiers

$0 – $1,999.99	3%
$2,000 – $9,999.99	4%
$10,000 – $15,999.99	5%
> $16,000.00	7%

Ad Groups	Day 1			Day 2			Day 3		
	Clicks	Cost	Total Sales	Clicks	Cost	Total Sales	Clicks	Cost	Total Sales
Book ads	76	$3.80	$79.66	81	$4.05	$84.97	91	$4.55	$95.59
Electronics	18	$1.26	$38.25	19	$1.33	$40.80	21	$1.47	$45.90
Toys	190	$19.00	$243.00	203	$22.33	$259.20	228	$22.80	$291.60
Computers	76	$4.18	$72.16	81	$4.46	$76.97	91	$5.01	$86.59
Music	75	$3.38	$71.57	80	$3.60	$76.34	90	$4.05	$85.88

Projected total sales: $16,484.58
Projected commission tier: 7.00%

Ad Groups	Projected Cost	Projected Earnings	Projected Return	CPC	EPC	RPC
Book ads	$124.00	$182.15	$58.15	$0.05	$0.07	$0.02
Electronics	$40.60	$87.47	$46.87	$0.07	$0.15	$0.08
Toys	$641.30	$555.66	–$85.64	$0.10	$0.09	–$0.01
Computers	$136.40	$165.00	$28.60	$0.06	$0.07	$0.01
Music	$110.25	$163.65	$53.40	$0.05	$0.07	$0.02
Totals	$1,052.55	$1,153.92	$187.01			

reveals, however, that you are only barely in the 7 percent tier, and Toys is your largest ad group in terms of volume. So, should you turn it off? Let's see what happens if you strike it out of your forecast (see Table 9.4).

The loss of your Toys ad group has dropped you down to the 5 percent commission level, and, as a result, your RPC for all your remaining campaigns has plummeted, your Computers ad group is now losing money (when previously it was making money), and your total return has dropped from $101.37 all the way down to $16.08.

Clearly, you should keep your Toys ad group running, not because it is making money on its own—it is not—but because it accounts for half your total sales, and without it you cannot hope to reach the 7 percent commission level. Neither can you tune the Toys ad group separately by lowering the bids or narrowing the scope of the keywords, as you are only barely above the $16,000 tier. In fact, you should probably raise your bid a little to be certain you do not fall short of your performance goal for the month. You could try tuning your ad text, but there may or may not be much room for improvement.

Your best course of action in this circumstance might be to think of additional product lines to advertise for BuyIt.com. If the site sells movies, clothing, baby accessories, and so forth, then a few more ad groups might place you deep enough into the 7 percent commission level to begin to slowly lower your bids in the Toys campaign without dropping you down to the 5 percent level and adversely affecting all your ad groups.

I will not put you to sleep by laying out all the possibilities for you. Just remember that when you have multiple ad groups supporting a campaign with performance goals, these ad groups are very dependent on each other. Sometimes you may need to take steps that seem counterintuitive at first, such as allowing your

Buylt.com Projection Worksheet

Table 9.4 Projection with Toys Ad Group Struck

Ad Groups	Day 1			Day 2			Day 3		
	Clicks	Cost	Total Sales	Clicks	Cost	Total Sales	Clicks	Cost	Total Sales
Book ads	76	$3.80	$79.66	81	$4.05	$84.97	91	$4.55	$95.59
Electronics	18	$1.26	$38.25	19	$1.33	$40.80	21	$1.47	$45.90
Toys	~~100~~	~~$19.00~~	~~$243.00~~	~~203~~	~~$22.33~~	~~$259.20~~	~~228~~	~~$22.80~~	~~$291.60~~
Computers	76	$4.18	$72.16	81	$4.46	$76.97	91	$5.01	$86.59
Music	75	$3.38	$71.57	80	$3.60	$76.34	90	$4.05	$85.88

Projected total sales: $8,546.58
Projected commission tier: 5.00%

Ad Groups	Projected Cost	Projected Earnings	Projected Return	CPC	EPC	RPC
Book ads	$124.00	$130.11	$6.11	$0.05	$0.05	$0.00
Electronics	$40.60	$62.48	$21.88	$0.07	$0.11	$0.04
Computers	$136.40	$117.86	–$18.54	$0.06	$0.05	–$0.01
Music	$110.25	$116.89	$6.64	$0.05	$0.05	$0.00
Totals	$411.25	$427.33	$34.62			

Toys campaign to keep running at a loss for the time being. And remember, as you work to tune your campaigns, however simple or complex they may be, your goal is always the same: to maximize your total return.

Maximizing Returns

Performance tuning is all about maximizing your returns, and if you remember to focus on your total return as you make your adjustments, you can be certain your campaigns are running at full efficiency. Performance tuning is not the only concern when working to ensure the best return on your dollar, though. Knowing and avoiding the common pitfalls and mistakes that search marketers make is also important to protecting your bottom line. This is why Chapter 10 focuses on avoiding common mistakes and recovering from your errors when you do make them.

Chapter 10

Dealing with Mistakes

You will not be doing affiliate advertising very long before you begin making mistakes. The purpose of this chapter is not to prevent you from ever making a mistake, but rather to alert you to the danger. Hopefully, you will avoid taking some backward steps as a result of reading this, but my main goal is to help you recognize and fix the mistakes that you do make as quickly and painlessly—I am speaking of your wallet now—as possible. The key is to watch carefully for the inevitable errors that will occur and also to learn from your mistakes and turn them into positive learning experiences; if you can do that, you'll be just fine.

COMMON MISTAKES

There are a number of common mistakes you can expect to run into sooner or later if you are in this business long enough. Here are some of the most common:

- Bidding mistakes
- Client compliance guidelines

- Bad links
- Changed or canceled program terms

Keep a close eye out for these types of mistakes and errors; if you identify and correct them as quickly as possible, you can limit the damage they might otherwise do to your bottom line. Let them slip by unnoticed, however, and they can quickly cause incalculable harm.

Bidding Blunders

Perhaps the most common mistakes are made in the bidding process. Predictably, these mistakes can be some of the most costly. Outrageous expenses are the obvious danger, but an error in bidding can hit you just as hard when it cuts your revenue instead. Let's start with your maximum bids, or maximum cost per click (CPC).

Maximum Bids. A mistake in setting or adjusting your maximum bid naturally carries with it the risk of inflating your costs, lowering your revenues, and generally ruining an otherwise beautiful day. It doesn't matter if the mistake is a typo—the search engines will not care—or a gross miscalculation on your part, the results will be equally painful. With a new campaign, the danger is especially great.

Any time you set or adjust your bids, you must double-check the amount for typos, and thoroughly think through your decisions. If you raise your bids, do so slowly, and be aware that the resulting increase in volume could be exponential. Double-check your maximum daily budget and imagine the worst: the entire amount spent, and your CPC at the full maximum. If you can live with that as a result (and that result is always a real possibility), then fine. If not, lower your maximum daily budget, or do not raise your bid quite as high.

Conversely, when you are lowering your bids, be aware that the drop in volume could also be exponential. If you believe you can make a successful campaign more profitable by lowering your bid and increasing your margins, by all means try it. But watch the results closely, because if the volume drops more steeply than you predicted, your earnings could drop beyond the amount that a wider margin could justify. Losing money that should have come in can hurt just as much as paying money out.

Above all, you must monitor your campaigns closely when you make changes to your maximum bids, and most especially when raising them. You should never raise your bids just before going to bed, out to dinner and a movie, or on a trip to the beach, for instance. Make sure that when you make these changes, you are able to monitor the results for at least a few hours. I have lost hundreds of dollars in just a few short hours because of a poorly placed bid, and it takes only a few brief distractions to turn a hundred-dollar mistake into a thousand-dollar one. If you have already made other plans that will demand your attention, make your bid changes when you are finished.

Maximum Daily Budget. My first truly costly mistake occurred on a campaign I created on a third-tier search engine I was trying out for the first time. This campaign was a duplicate, essentially, of a campaign I had been running on Google, and my earnings per click for that campaign were roughly 16 cents. I set my maximum bid at a conservative 10 cents per click, and then I set my maximum daily budget at about $3,000. This was the same as the daily budget for my campaign on Google, and Google had never exhausted this amount in a single day. Considering my expected

EPC of 16 cents, I was not concerned about the remote possibility that this new search engine could exhaust this amount in a single day.

I checked in on the new campaign about an hour after I started it, and I was delighted to see that my actual cost per click was a mere 3 cents, and that I had already received hundreds of clicks. True, part of me already new that if the volume was that high, I should lower my budget or turn off my campaign and wait until my actual commissions began to be recorded before I went any further. However, based on the fact that my nearly identical campaign on Google was earning over 16 cents per click, and my costs on this new campaign were only 3 cents per click, I reasoned that even if the traffic from this new search engine performed just half as well, I would still make a tidy profit. I decided to let it ride.

A few hours after that, I began monitoring commissions (this particular affiliate program usually posted commissions within about four hours of the actual event). There was nothing. Not one dime. I rushed back to the new campaign, already in considerable distress, and discovered the clicks reported already numbered in the thousands (and the past hour or two was likely not yet included). I turned the campaign off immediately, and then I watched. Eventually, some commissions did begin to post. I made roughly $300, in fact. The final total number of clicks I received was almost 9,000, however, and even at just 3 cents per click, I had spent close to $3,000. My losses were enormous. I had only just begun search marketing, and my net profit to date at the time was only a few hundred dollars. My error had put me thousands of dollars in the red, and I very nearly gave up on search marketing—and the millions of dollars I have made since.

I have since made even costlier mistakes (a $20,000 loss in one day is my current record), and although I now earn enough to survive even a very costly mistake or two, it never feels good to part with so much money and get nothing in return. So remember, *when you set your daily maximum, never set it higher than the amount you are willing to lose.*

Another thing to keep in mind is this: The daily maximum you set can be exceeded—sometimes by quite a bit—if the volume of traffic is high enough. Most search engines will guarantee only that your average daily budget at the end of the month will not exceed your limit. This means that in a single day, you can—in theory—go 30 times over your daily budget and still meet the site's guarantee if your traffic for the next 29 days shuts down or slows to a trickle. I am not saying you are likely to ever have your daily budget exceeded by a factor of 30. I am only saying that you should be aware that it is technically possible.

My worst such experience to date was a new campaign I set up on a popular search engine that had its daily budget of $100 exceeded sixfold in just a few hours. The site was kind enough to credit back to me a portion of this amount, but it happened again almost immediately afterward before it finally sank into my head that the daily budget maximum was not really a daily limitation.

This does not mean that your daily budget limits are meaningless. For the majority of your campaigns—those with light to medium traffic volume—the daily budget should work quite well on a daily basis. It is only for high-volume campaigns, where the traffic is generated quickly enough to reach your limit in minutes rather than hours, that huge excesses may occur. The key to avoiding this is to always use the traffic estimators provided by most search engines when creating or editing campaigns.

You can find Google's traffic estimator, for instance, while editing your keywords. Before you save changes, click on "Estimate Search Traffic" instead (see Figure 10.1).

If you see an unusually high estimated traffic volume, as shown in Figure 10.2, you should proceed with the utmost caution.

Figure 10.1 Google's Traffic Estimator
Source: Screenshots © Google Inc. and are used with permission.

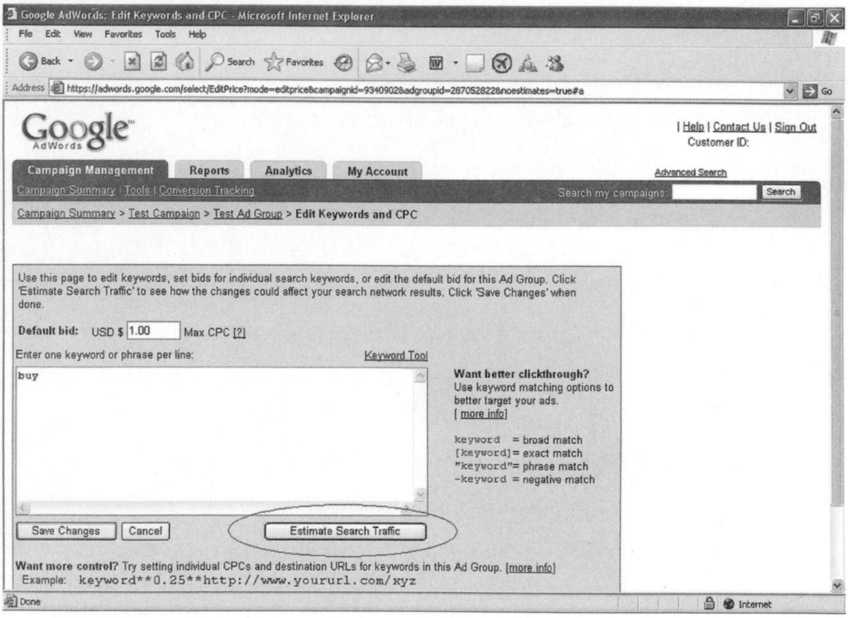

If the estimator is predicting high click volumes, you should consider turning the campaign off manually within the first 15 to 30 minutes and waiting for the results before deciding whether to continue. If the volume is not overly high—or if it is high but your RPC indicates the campaign is comfortably profitable—then you may turn the campaign back on without much concern for your daily budget maximum. If the volume is very high and your RPC is not showing a comfortable margin, then you will need to continue manually running the campaign in short spurts until your performance-tuning efforts either make the campaign profitable or fail to do so.

Client Compliance Guidelines

Here is a mistake that I made several times before it finally caught up to me, and I hadn't even realized what I had done. Every affil-

Figure 10.2 Example of High Estimated Traffic
Source: Screenshots © Google Inc. and are used with permission.

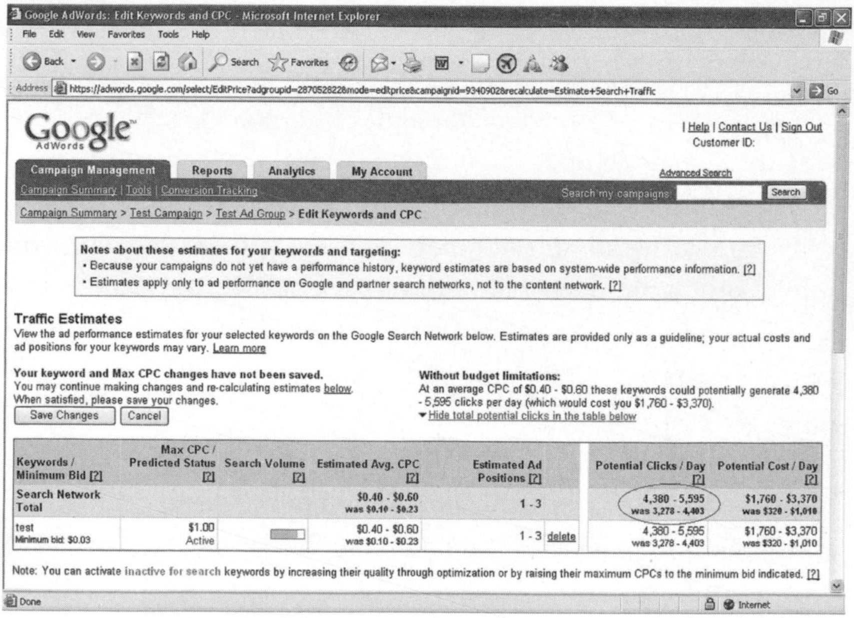

iate program you join has terms and conditions. Some are more complicated than others, but it is important to read them all. When I started, I made the mistake of assuming, after putting myself to sleep reading a couple of these, that they were all pretty much the same—and pretty much irrelevant to me and my simple advertising model. I didn't even have a web site, after all. So how could I possibly offend my clients?

Well, I found out the hard way that these terms and conditions are *not* all the same. In particular, as a search marketer, you want to look for two things:

1. Does the client prohibit search marketing entirely?
2. Does the client have a negative keyword list or a prohibition against using their company's registered trademarks?

I had several campaigns in my early months that either should not have been marketed on search engines at all or should not have been marketed for certain keywords and trademarks. It is a very unpleasant experience to believe you are earning good money on several different campaigns and then to start receiving cease-and-desist letters, warning you not only to turn off your campaign, but that your commissions may be forfeited.

Be forewarned. It doesn't matter whose affiliate program you are working with, they are all serious about their terms and conditions. Make sure you know what is and isn't allowed before you start working with a new affiliate program.

Bad Links

Another common error that can cost you money: bad destination links. There are two kinds of destination link errors that you want to watch out for.

1. Broken links
2. Missing tracking code

Broken Links. Broken destination links are links that, because of a typo or other error, do not lead anywhere. These are typically the easiest to catch and the least likely to cost you a lot of money, but they can cost you some, so watch out. The total lack of reporting information for your click traffic on the affiliate side is one big tip-off that something is wrong. Although, if you have more than one ad but only one is broken, you won't have the benefit of this big clue. Oftentimes the search engine itself will catch this error quickly and shut off the broken ad, but it won't be refunding your money, so don't wait for the search engine to do your job for you. Every new ad you write, and every existing ad you edit, must be tested immediately by clicking on it yourself. If you don't wind up where you wanted to go, fix it.

Missing Tracking Code. Missing or incorrect tracking codes from your destination links can be harder to catch, and as a result they can go unnoticed longer, causing greater financial pain than a simple broken link might. As with broken links, a complete lack of reporting data on click traffic might alert you, but only if none of your ads for the campaign are working right. Missing or incorrect tracking codes might not prevent your ad from sending customers to the correct site, so just clicking on the ad won't always catch the problem. Even worse, search engines care only that your ad leads customers where it says it will, not whether it is tracked correctly. As a result, you cannot count on them to turn off these problem ads.

If you have multiple ads and only one or two are broken, you might never notice anything more than poor campaign performance, and you might possibly even shut down campaigns that could have been successful. Watch your click traffic closely with new ads. The click volume reported by the search engine and the affiliate program should roughly approximate each other (they will rarely sync up completely, as reporting cycles and reporting delays may differ). If the affiliate program consistently reports fewer clicks than your search engines report, missing tracking code in one or more of your ads' destination links is the likely culprit.

Editing or Deleting Successful Ads

I have mentioned this before, of course, but it bears repeating here. Ad history is an important element of some—if not all—paid search algorithms. When editing or deleting ads, take care that you are working on the correct ad and that the ad does, in fact, need improving. Accidentally editing or deleting a successful ad can be a painful experience that can take a campaign days, weeks, or even months to recover from. Re-creating the ad exactly will, in most cases, return your campaign to its previous level of performance, but only over time.

Changed or Canceled Program Terms

As you join more and more affiliate programs, staying with some and abandoning others, you will begin to notice a steady stream of e-mails regarding these programs. If you are not fastidious when it comes to canceling your participation for programs you have given up on, these notices can become quite a nuisance. It is very important, however, that you read these notices to ascertain whether they will impact you.

A missed cancellation notice means you will pay for ads with no hope of them generating revenue until you discover your mistake and turn off your campaign. Individual links and tracking codes may also be canceled and will cost you just as much if you fail to read the e-mail sent to alert you.

Program changes can be just as bad. A sudden drop in payouts could turn a winning campaign into a losing one overnight. Even an increase in payouts can hurt you if you don't know about it. The competition will raise their bids accordingly, but your own bids will remain the same, likely resulting in a big drop in click volume as other ads begin running more often and in higher positions than yours.

Many of the e-mails you receive from affiliate programs and affiliate networks will have little or no impact on your business, but if you do not take the time to read each one, you will inevitably get burned.

LEARNING FROM MISTAKES

My uncle once shared with me an excellent piece of advice. "Tony, if you don't learn from your mistakes, it's like paying for your college tuition and then sleeping through your classes." (Coincidentally, falling asleep in class was a recurring problem of mine.) In other words, the pain of our mistakes is the cost of our tuition in life, but it can be worth the pain if we pay attention to those mistakes and learn something from them. I thought this was a mildly intelligent statement, and I was mildly impressed, but then he went one step further. "If you can learn from someone else's mistakes, Tony, it's like having them pay your tuition for you."

I thought this was nothing short of brilliant, and I have tried ever since to watch other people, to learn from their mistakes, and to seek their advice. Sadly, I have still had to pay much of my own tuition at the school of hard knocks, but not nearly as much as I might have had I not discovered long ago to learn from others' experiences as much as is humanly possible. My hope is that by sharing with you some of the mistakes I have made in this business and giving my advice on what to look out for, my painful experiences will pay some of your own tuition. If you allow yourself to learn from my mistakes, perhaps your own road to success will offer a few less bumps along the way.

Chapter 11

Growing Your Business: A Call to Action

Achieving success in affiliate marketing is a two-step process. The first step actually consists of four activities: Get your foot in the door; become proficient at writing ads; identify some affiliate programs that are in demand and that you show some proficiency in promoting; and develop some successful search marketing campaigns for those programs. The second step is to those successful campaigns and to grow them. Exactly how to take that second step and to make your business grow successfully is the subject of this chapter.

SEARCHING FOR NEW OPPORTUNITIES

The Internet is still the modern gold rush of our time, and it promises to remain so indefinitely. Affiliate advertising and search marketing are, in my own opinion, the easiest way for anyone with a computer to share in the almost limitless opportunities that still abound online. But you will have to search for these opportunities and recognize the ones that hold the most promise for you as an individual. Recognizing these opportunities will be the key to your success.

Finding New Campaigns and Affiliate Programs

While a small number of readers may experience instant success with the first campaign they try, most will struggle through several or more before fully developing the skills they need to recognize which campaigns hold the most potential for them, personally, and to unlock that potential. Whether you struggle for a while or find success quickly, remember to always keep searching for the next successful campaign.

When you have been in this business for a few years, as I have, you will learn that even the most successful campaigns can dry up, suffer from program changes and cancellations, or be overtaken by a skilled competitor. The key to long-term success and security is the steady addition of new successful campaigns and new revenue streams to replace those that you will occasionally lose.

Your first big success may bring with it the temptation stop the tedious search for new campaigns, but you will put yourself and your career as a search marketer in serious jeopardy if you give in to this temptation. The almost inevitable end to most campaigns, when they come, is hard enough to face. But without other successful campaigns to ensure your financial security and maintain your confidence, the loss of a really successful campaign can be a terrible blow both financially and emotionally. You have a responsibility to yourself to mitigate this possibility by continually seeking new affiliate program opportunities.

Expanding Existing Campaigns

It's tempting to sit back once you have had a little success. You're making a few dollars, you're getting a few checks in the mail—or deposited directly into your bank account—and it's easy to just sit back and watch the money roll in. But in many ways, the thing that separates successful marketers from the just so-so ones is persistence. Just because your existing campaign is already a success does not mean that it cannot still be a source of additional revenue. Once a campaign becomes a success, it deserves some extra attention, as it is now a proven revenue generator. Can you think of additional keywords to add to appropriate ad groups within the campaign? Are you marketing all of the affiliate program's products and/or services? Can you create additional ad groups to market these other products and services?

Some of my most successful campaigns started relatively small, with modest returns, and grew only when I began expanding the overall campaign with new ad groups to promote additional products and services I had not yet advertised. If you are meeting with some success promoting a few products for, as an example, Amazon.com or eBay, why not take advantage of their broad range of products and proven earning potential and try to advertise additional items? These affiliate programs have performance tiers that pay higher commissions for higher levels of volume, and adding additional ad groups can often have an exponential effect on your total return.

Revisiting Failed Campaigns

Early in your search marketing career—and perhaps even later in it—you can be expected to fail with some campaigns that your developing skill set might someday be able to turn into a success. When you abandon a campaign that you failed to make profitable, you should never consider that campaign forever retired. From time to time, as you judge your skills to have improved significantly in one or more areas, you should reexamine your old campaigns to see whether you can make successes out of some former failures now that you possess the knowledge and skill that you were then lacking. If you recognize a campaign that failed for some reason unknown to you at the time—but that you now think you understand—by all means resurrect the campaign to see if, in fact, you can now make it profitable.

For example, as you look over your old campaigns you might notice an ad for downloading software that you failed to mention was free. The power of the word *free* (when appropriate) in paid search advertising may have been unknown or underestimated by you when you first wrote this ad. Restarting the campaign with a new ad highlighting "Free Download" might be all it takes to turn an old loser into a winner. Perhaps you will notice baseball equipment keywords that failed to maintain high enough click-through rates to remain active on Google. Your more experienced eye might recognize that keywords like *bat*, *glove*, *helmet*, and so forth are far too general and should be changed to *batting helmet* and *baseball bat*. Perhaps *glove* could be expanded into several more-descriptive phrases such as *batting glove*, *ball glove*, and *baseball glove*. Negative keywords, like *souvenir*, might weed out people looking for small souvenir baseball bats that your affiliate program doesn't sell at all.

The point is, many of the things you will learn as you grow your business will be lessons that could save some of your earlier campaigns if applied to them. Make a habit of spending a few hours every three months or so to reexamine your old campaigns with an eye toward finding one or two that might have failed for lack of some piece of knowledge or skill that you now possess. Try to restart or rebuild those campaigns using your new talents. Sometimes, the rewards will surprise you.

REINVESTING PROFITS TO SUPPORT FUTURE GROWTH

A successful search marketing business is a growing search marketing business. Make sure that you have the cash on hand to support that growth. More than once in the early stages of my business, I was forced to turn off lucrative campaigns because my click volume grew unexpectedly and devoured all my available cash. Considering the fact that, in some cases, I was making as much as five times what I was able to spend, my inability to keep a steady supply of cash flowing into this moneymaking machine was quite distressing. At one point, I was unable to fund a campaign for almost 30 days that was capable of converting as much as $500 a day into a $2,500 per day return. It simply took all the money I had, leaving me with no money to purchase new clicks and forcing me to wait until my next check before I could fund the successful campaign again.

Remember, most affiliate networks and programs will not pay out commissions until near the end of the month after you earn them. Some, such as Amazon.com and Barnes & Noble, pay out commissions in the month after the quarter in which you earn your commissions. This can mean a wait of between roughly 45 and 105 days before you see the return on your advertising investment. Without careful planning—and sometimes even with it—it is easy for a successful campaign's demands to outstrip your resources.

Planning Ahead

Calculate how much you are spending on a daily basis for each campaign. Multiply that figure by 60 (i.e., a two-month supply), and you have the bare minimum amount of cash you should have on hand to operate each campaign. If some campaigns show signs of steady growth, you may need to try and keep even more cash on hand.

I do not suggest that you meet this cash requirement by investing any more of your own money than you would otherwise feel comfortable risking, but I do strongly advise that when it comes time to take cash out of the business—that's why we are doing this, after all, to make money—that you be very disciplined about how much you take. Don't let your cash reserves fall below that 60-day minimum just because you really want a new motorcycle this month and it's really just 30 days to your next affiliate check anyway. Big opportunities can come—and go—quickly, and if one of your campaigns suddenly hits its stride, it could quickly outpace your ability to fund it. You will be forced to sit on the sidelines waiting for your next check to arrive, knowing that if you had only left more cash on hand, you would be raking in hundreds, perhaps even thousands, more dollars.

Allocating Scarce Resources

There may, of course, be times when even careful planning cannot guarantee you will have all the cash you need. If the success of one or more campaigns appears poised to outstrip your ability to keep these campaigns funded, you should be prepared to make some hard decisions. I have, in the past, made the mistake of simply letting all my campaigns run until the money runs out, and then shutting off all these campaigns until my affiliate payments arrive and I have the money to start them again. You might ask, "What is the problem with this approach?" The problem is, not all campaigns are created equal, and some campaigns require relatively large investments for small returns. Consider Table 11.1.

Let's say that at the beginning of November you have only $8,000 left to spend on advertising, and you don't expect your next check to arrive until sometime after November 20. Looking back at your October campaign expenditures, you can see that you might just make it to November 20 without running out of money. Your Jungle.com campaign, however, suddenly starts to enjoy nearly twice as many clicks per day as it once did, and its projected RPC appears to remain relatively unchanged (i.e., you are making as much per dollar spent as you were last month on

Table 11.1 Previous Month's Campaign Expenses and Earnings

Campaign Expenses and Returns

October Figures

	Total Cost	Total Commissions	Net Return
Munster Jobs	$4,520.04	$5,721.04	$1,201.00
Jungle.com	$4,809.57	$12,604.61	$7,795.04
BuyIt.com	$1,006.08	$1,213.50	$207.42
Schoolmates.com	$598.77	$684.10	$85.33

this campaign). You can see now that you do not have enough money to keep all these campaigns running, but which ones should you shut off?

To answer this question, you must determine which campaigns are giving you the highest return on your dollar. The best measurement in this case would be to examine your net return as a percentage of money invested by performing a simple calculation:

Net return ÷ commissions = net return as a percentage

In Table 11.2, I have made these calculations for you already. Let's examine the results.

Obviously, you are getting the best return on your Jungle.com campaign, and you should be very excited that this campaign appears to be taking off. In fact, you are getting very good returns from all these campaigns, and it is really too bad that you will be forced to turn off some or all of them. You need to save about $4,000 (at a minimum) to ensure that you can keep your Jungle .com campaign funded. You could save the entire amount by simply pausing your Munster Jobs campaign, but with a net return of

Table 11.2 Comparing Campaign Performances

Comparison of Campaign Performances
October Figures

	Total Cost	Commissions	Net Return	Net Return as a Percentage
Munster Jobs	$4,520.04	$5,721.04	$1,201.00	21%
Jungle.com	$4,809.57	$12,604.61	$7,795.04	62%
BuyIt.com	$1,006.08	$1,213.50	$207.42	17%
Schoolmates.com	$598.77	$684.10	$85.33	12%

21 percent, you don't want to touch that campaign, either, unless you have to.

The obvious choice is Schoolmates.com, as it is returning only 12 percent, but pausing this campaign for the month will save you only $598. You could add BuyIt.com to your list, but you would still be saving only about $1,600. What do you do? Well, you don't want to pause your Munster Jobs campaign, because it is getting your second-highest-percentage return, but if you leave it running the way it is—even if you shut off the others—your top-performing campaign will run out of money.

The answer in this case would be to pause the other two campaigns and to set a daily budget of $66 ($2000 per month) on your Munster Jobs campaign. This should save you $2,500 on your Munster Jobs campaign and still allow you to get as much traffic as you can afford for this high-performing campaign. Pausing the other two campaigns will save you another $1,600, for a total of about $4,100 this month, giving you just a little more than you think you might need to fully fund your top-performing campaign, Jungle.com. The result will be an additional $4,000 or so invested in the Jungle.com campaign at 62 percent, earning you a net profit of $2,480. Had you invested that same $4,000 into your lower-performing campaigns, your net profit on that investment would have been only about $800.

To sum it all up as simply as possible, if you don't have enough money to fund all your successful campaigns, then fund the best performer(s) first. Put your money where it will earn the highest return, and don't fund your less successful campaign(s) until you have more than enough money to fund the better-performing campaign(s) first. Never forget about that bottom line.

THE AFFILIATE MILLIONS WEB SITE

The Affiliate Millions web site can be a valuable tool for you as you start to grow your business. I keep this site up-to-date and current with all the information and tools you'll need to make your search marketing business a success. Just visit us at www .AffiliateMillions.com and check out all we have to offer.

Quick Start Guide

My Quick Start Guide on the Affiliate Millions web site is the fastest and easiest way to get your search marketing business started, walking you through each and every step with helpful advice and direct links to the partners and clients you'll need to develop relationships with, such as affiliate networks, search and content networks, and more. This guide offers informative advice to help you decide whether to set up your own web site or directly market your client's web sites instead, and it provides you with all the tools you need to get started.

Affiliate Networks

AffiliateMillions.com always has an updated list of all the best affiliate networks on the Web—all on one convenient page. We offer tips on which programs are hot and which are not. Seasonal affiliate program opportunities are prominently featured, as well as online marketing trends that you'll want to take advantage of. You'll find everything you need to locate and join the affiliate programs that are right for you.

Search Engines and Content Networks

At AffiliateMillions.com, there's an up-to-date list of all the biggest search engines and content networks you'll want to advertise with. We let you know which engines still use the old pay-for-placement model and which ones offer the performance-based paid search algorithms that allow a savvy ad writer to excel. We offer tips on how to get the most out of your advertising budget, and we give you specific advice on each individual search engine's strengths.

Purchasing Domain Names

Purchasing domain names is easy at AffiliateMillions.com. We offer a variety of choices for finding and buying the perfect domain name for you, whether you need to purchase a currently registered name on the aftermarket or register a brand-new name for the first time. Detailed information on pricing and services helps you find the right company fast.

Web Hosting

If you decide to develop your own web site, AffiliateMillions.com has a comprehensive and up-to-date list of Web hosting companies to choose from across a wide spectrum of price and service points. You'll find exactly what you need, and fast.

Web Site Templates (and Other Tools)

Do you prefer the web site model for your search marketing business but are unwilling or unable to develop your own web site? AffiliateMillions.com has free, completed web site templates for educational sites, news sites, and more. These sites are attractive, functional, and ready to go. Just replace the existing ad links in the code with your own ads and links from the affiliate programs you've joined. Then publish the site with the help of your Web hosting company and start advertising your site online immediately.

We are constantly working to provide a variety of other tools, worksheets, and so forth to help you make your business a success.

Affiliate Millions Newsletter

Don't forget to sign up for the free *Affiliate Millions* newsletter when you visit our site. Receive regular tips and updates on the hottest new affiliate programs, paid search changes and opportunities, and industry news and events. We offer additional advice and tips for working at home and employing yourself in your own business. Since you'll probably be pursuing your business at home, you'll want to learn about tax regulations and business designations for self-employed individuals, and you'll find out about them in Chapter 12.

Chapter 12

Working at Home:
Legal and Tax Requirements

Hopefully, your affiliate advertising activities will be successful enough that you'll be able to support yourself, at least part-time if not full-time. In any event, you'll have started your own online business, and running your own business raises a host of other issues.

One of the things I've learned from quitting my day job and supporting myself is that I need to observe some business practices and rules that go along with being self-employed. This kind of stuff isn't very sexy. It will help you avoid trouble that can quickly sidetrack your business, get you into trouble with your spouse and the government, and make your life very difficult, to say the least. When you're lucky enough to start making income on a regular basis from affiliate advertising, start planning the type of business you want to run, and get in the habit of keeping accurate records so you can pay your taxes.

SELF-EMPLOYMENT AND OWNING YOUR OWN BUSINESS

You don't have to make 100 percent of your income from affiliate marketing or advertising in order to be considered self-employed. If you do this work part-time in addition to your regular day job, the Internal Revenue Service (IRS) will consider you self-employed.

Your conception of what it means to be self-employed probably isn't quite the same as it is for the government. You probably think you're just a lone entrepreneur sitting at a computer somewhere, placing ads and managing campaigns. The government, however, wants your operation to fall into a more specific designation than just "someone working at home." Specifically, it wants businesses to be categorized by *general designations*, some of which are described in the sections that follow: sole proprietorships, corporations, limited liability companies, or partnerships.

> **TIP:** A New Jersey tax firm has created a free online utility that leads you step-by-step through the process of determining what form your company should take. Check out Choose the Best Legal Entity for your business at www.taxesq.com and click on "Choose the Best Legal Entity for your Business."

Sole Proprietorship

A sole proprietorship is the simplest form of business (versus a more elaborate form such as a corporation). You are the sole person responsible for the business; you don't have a board of directors; and you own all the assets. If you weren't present, the business wouldn't exist, either. As a sole proprietor, you report income and expenses on your personal tax return.

One of the big advantages of a sole proprietorship is that you don't need an accountant or lawyer to help you form the business (though it helps), and you certainly don't have to answer to partners or stockholders. To declare a sole proprietorship, you may have to file an application; check with your local county clerk.

Corporation

Why incorporate? Protection from liability against debt or other problems is one of the main incentives. When you form a corporation, you issue stock, which belongs to shareholders. You do not need to have more than one owner, or shareholder, to incorporate. When you incorporate, you separate the owner or owners of the business from the business itself. The owners and managers are thus shielded, to a degree, from liability in case someone sues your corporation or you run into debt. Incorporation is a complex undertaking. You should hire a lawyer to explain the options and benefits of incorporating in your individual state and to file papers in order to meet the regulations provided by both the federal and state agencies that oversee corporations.

Another reason for incorporating is the fact that corporations can take special deductions that other forms of business cannot. For instance, I set up an S corporation for myself because I gained the ability to set up a SEP retirement account and to deduct contributions I made to it. Again, though, you should consult a lawyer, and perhaps an accountant, to determine the best course of action for you and your business.

Limited Liability Company

A limited liability company (LLC) is a good alternative for individual business owners who want to protect themselves against liability without incurring the complexities of incorporation. In an LLC, income and losses are shared by the individual investors, who are known as *members*. Laws vary from state to state, so you'll still need an attorney to answer your questions, to prepare forms, and to file them properly.

Partnership

If you and your spouse, or you and a friend, do your affiliate marketing together, you may want to make your business a formal partnership. A partnership is a legal designation that spells out how much of the business each partner owns, so they can avoid conflicts. Conversely, each partner also shares in the liability in case of losses—and each has to pay a share of the taxes that are due as well.

NOTE: This chapter is just a starting point for understanding the legal requirements of your business. There's no substitute for consulting an attorney who can help you prepare privacy statements, guide you through the incorporation process, and help you register a trademark for your business name if you want to protect it in the marketplace. Do a search for "e-commerce attorney" on Google or in Yahoo!'s directory to find a lawyer who specializes in doing business on the Internet.

LICENSING AND LEGAL CONSIDERATIONS

As an experienced affiliate advertiser, you're used to following rules. You need to follow the rules established by your search and content networks, your affiliate networks, and your advertisers. It's not a great leap to observing the rules and procedures set forth by the IRS and by your state and local municipality.

Obtaining a Business License

Before you set up your home office and start working out of your home, you should check to make certain that you aren't violating the law by doing so. Some municipalities prohibit businesses from being run in residential areas. In truth, it's difficult to deduct business activity of the sort discussed in this book, which mostly involves sitting at your computer for periods of time. But I'm not going to tell you to break the law, either. You should, at the very least, know what regulations you need to comply with. Some local regulations cover the following:

- *Business taxes.* Some cities tax businesses for the use of things like office furniture and computer equipment.
- *Business name.* If your company's name is different from your own name, you may be required to submit a Doing Business As (DBA) certificate that identifies you as the owner. You might even be required to publish a notice in your local newspaper stating that you have submitted this certificate. Visit or call your city or county clerk's office to find out more.
- *Business license.* Some states or local governments may require you to obtain a business license. Visit or call your city or county clerk's office to find out more.

TIP: It can be difficult to keep track of all the business regulations you need to comply with. One of the best resources available is the Small Business Administration's web site (www.sba.gov), which includes licensing information for individual U.S. states as well as tips and advice on business planning, taxes, and legal aspects of starting a business.

Obtaining Identification Numbers

You need an ID number when you obtain a driver's license. You also need some kind of identification number when you run your own business. The good news is you probably already have one of the required numbers. The IRS requires you to have a Taxpayer Identification Number (TIN). A TIN can be one of the following:

- A social security number
- An Employer Identification Number (EIN)
- An Individual Taxpayer Identification Number (ITIN)

You might also need a state tax ID number; check with your individual state's department of revenue (if you have one) to find out how to do this. A tax ID number is important if you plan to sell tangible goods and you need to buy them for resale: Your supplier might ask you for one. Since you're an affiliate marketer, however, a tax ID number is of secondary importance.

TAXES AND ACCOUNTING

If you are a self-employed individual and you have annual earnings of $400 or more, you are subject to the self-employment tax. You are also required to fill out several different tax forms with which you may be unfamiliar. These include the following:

- Schedule SE to Form 1040
- Schedule C or C-EZ, on which you report income and expenses
- Form 1040-ES, on which you estimate and pay your self-employment tax

Filling out all these forms is something you can definitely handle on your own if you have the time and some aptitude for math (and if you are successful at affiliate advertising, you probably do). But just because you *can* do it yourself doesn't mean that you *should*. I strongly recommend hiring an accountant to do your taxes, at least for the first year, so you can be sure this task is done right. Even if you have one of those high-tech electronic tax preparation programs available, you probably won't do things in the same way as a professional. You should strongly consider hiring a tax expert to help you when you start filing self-employment taxes.

You probably won't have to hire an accountant immediately. If you use computer software to keep your books, you can handle your own record keeping. I didn't hire an accountant until after I had two very successful years in my business.

Paying Quarterly Taxes

One of the biggest practical changes I had to make when I quit my day job and started working at home involved taxes. Instead of having my employer withhold taxes from each of my paychecks during the year, I have to pay taxes on a quarterly basis. I estimate the amount of tax I am going to have to pay at tax time and divide that by four; the result is a quarterly payment I send the IRS and my state tax agency. This is just one of the general practices all self-employed businesspeople encounter: When it comes to taxes, it pays to plan ahead rather than doing things at the last minute.

This is where a professional tax expert can come in handy: This person can estimate the amount you need to pay each quarter and provide you with the forms you need to do it. If you are still a do-it-yourselfer when it comes to taxes, you can get the forms from the IRS and your state tax agency.

> **TIP:** The IRS puts out a publication called *Tax Withholding and Estimated Tax* (Publication 505) that will provide you with basic information about paying your estimated taxes on a quarterly basis. You can access it online at www.irs.gov/pub/irs-pdf/p505.pdf.

Keeping Good Financial Records

You don't need to be a professional bookkeeper to keep the sort of financial records that will help you get all the deductions you need at tax time. When you start reading instructions about different types of bookkeeping or accounting methods, you start hearing about terms like *cash basis accounting* and *accrual-basis accounting*. It all boils down to recording your income from purchases, your expenses (for the most part, your clicks), and any expenses you have for equipment and housing related to your business (e.g., utilities). Using an accounting software program like Quicken or QuickBooks should make the process easier.

In most businesses, you'll encounter expenses when you purchase merchandise in order to resell it. In the case of affiliate advertising, you aren't reselling, exactly, but you do have to pay for a lot of clicks in order to earn a fee from a purchase. Google's AdWords, MSN's adCenter, and other search and content providers do keep records of what you have been charged for clicks. Take advantage of these records to double-check your own figures for advertising expenses.

> **TIP:** For my own part, I print out a quarterly income/expense report generated by QuickBooks (I used to use Quicken) so I can calculate my quarterly estimated income tax payments.

Before I incorporated my own business, I used the popular personal finance software called Quicken to track income and expenses. Since incorporating, I moved to a more business-oriented software program, QuickBooks.

> **TIP:** Both Quicken and QuickBooks are available on the Web. You can find out more about Quicken at http://quicken.intuit.com. QuickBooks'

home page is at http://quickbooks.intuit.com. QuickBooks gives you two options for how to use its software: You can download or purchase the program and install it on your computer; or you can visit the Quick-Books online web site (http://oe.quickbooks.com) and sign up to use the program on the Web. That way, you can access your data from any computer connected to the Internet.

Table 12.1 lists some of the most popular accounting software packages and where you can find them on the Web. The main features of each are briefly summarized as well.

Track Those Deductions!

The difficult part about starting a business, from a tax standpoint, is that you have to observe so many new and different rules and procedures. One good thing, though, is the fact that you can take

Table 12.1 Accounting Programs for Small Business Owners

Program	Versions Available	Manufacturer & URL	Features
Microsoft Money	Essentials, Deluxe, Premium, Home, and Business	Microsoft (http://www .microsoft.com/ money)	Windows-only; supports the QFX files issued by banks for downloaded files
Peachtree Accounting	First Accounting, Pro Accounting, Complete Accounting, Premium Accounting, and Quantum Accounting	Sage Software (http://www .peachtree.com)	Provides demo version you can download; pro version includes inventory and analysis features
Quicken	Basic, Deluxe, Premier, Home, and Business	Intuit (http://quicken .intuit.com)	Comes in both Macintosh and Windows versions

more deductions than you can as an individual. Deductible expenses you might encounter in the type of business examined in this book include the following:

- *Computer equipment.* If your computer equipment is used solely or partly for your business activities, you may be able to deduct a portion for your business use.
- *Internet access.* Your monthly Internet access fee may be deductible, at least in part, because you use the Internet for all or part of your income.
- *Usage fees.* The fees you paid to join AdWords, MSN, and other services, or any fees they charge you, are deductible as business expenses.
- *Phone fees.* Chances are you use your land-line phone or your cell phone for business purposes. You can deduct the portion that applies to your business. (This may be an incentive for you to obtain a phone line that is dedicated to business use, in fact.)
- *Utilities.* Electricity is the big one you use, but gas for heating, water, and other utilities that you need to operate your home office are eligible, at least in part. (Check with your tax professional.)
- *Mortgage and taxes.* If your office is at home and you work primarily in your residence, you may be able to deduct that part of your mortgage and expenses related to your business. For example, if your office comprises one-eighth of your house, you may be able to deduct one-eighth of your mortgage and property taxes.

The fact that you need equipment such as modems, laptops, desktop computers, printers, and fax machines to do business means you need to consider depreciating that equipment. When you depreciate an item, you calculate its expense when spread out over its expected life span. In other words, you estimate how many years you are planning to use the item and divide the purchase price by the number of years. Computer equipment doesn't last very many years, as a general rule, and if you can't keep track of the deduction year after year, you may be able to deduct the purchase price all at once.

It's worth tracking your business deductions for reasons that should be obvious: The more money you can keep for yourself instead of turning it over to the government is money you can use to join more affiliate programs, take out more ads, and so on.

> **TIP:** The IRS has a site called One-Stop Resource for the Self-Employed at www.irs.gov/businesses/small/index.html. You'll find definitions of the different business types and information about fulfilling your tax requirements, too.

FINDING SPACE

When you work in the same space where your kids play and do their homework and where you and your spouse live and entertain guests, challenges arise related to your physical work area. Even if your work involves only sitting at your computer and talking on the phone occasionally, it's important to separate your work area from your home life. It is stressful when you're talking on the phone to a representative from an affiliate network and your kids are playing in the background playing and continually coming to you with requests. It also affects the other members of your family, who see you as working all the time even when you are in their midst. If you are able to close your door and work in private, when you come out they'll have your undivided attention.

Setting aside a work area in your home—a room that is solely devoted to business activities—also has important tax implications. You can deduct the expenses associated with equipping and running your home office. If your home has eight rooms and one of those is dedicated office space (i.e., you use that office 100 percent for business purposes), you may be able to take a deduction on your tax return. For instance, in this example you may be able to deduct one-eighth of your utilities because your office comprises one-eighth of your home. (Check with your tax preparer or accountant to make sure.)

> **TIP:** Setting up a separate phone line dedicated solely to your business will cost you more per month. But it can help your business. Your bank might require a business phone number in order for you to open a business checking account. Once you have a business phone number, you can advertise in your local phone book. It's not something you probably need to do if your business is solely devoted to affiliate marketing. But if you provide consulting services or branch out into a sales business, advertising in the phone book is an effective tool for expanding your customer base.

This chapter has offered you a glimpse of one of the benefits you'll have if you stick with affiliate advertising, if you work at it, and if you achieve success. It's called *independence*. You free yourself from dependence on an employer. But with independence comes the responsibility of running your own business. You are responsible for keeping financial records, for paying estimated taxes on a quarterly basis, and for equipping a home office with the equipment you need. For many people, such independence is a dream come true. It certainly has been for me. One of my current dreams is to help people like you achieve your own goals through affiliate advertising. I wish you luck, and I encourage you to visit my web site, www.AffiliateMillions.com, where you'll find up-to-date information, tips, tools, and additional instructions on how to make your own dream a reality.

Appendix

Affiliate Advertising Resources

This book focuses on affiliate advertising through search and content networks because that's my own bread-and-butter activity. I think it gives you a great way to get started in the field. Once you start to build a steady source of income through placing search ads, you may want to branch out to try other types of affiliate advertising. This appendix offers some other affiliate programs you may want to check out and some sources of support you may want to take advantage of so you can be even more successful.

RESOURCES FOR AFFILIATE MARKETERS

Affiliate Millions
www.AffiliateMillions.com

Of course, the number-one resource I can recommend to you is my own web site, www.AffiliateMillions.com. This site is intended to be a central location from which to find affiliate networks and program recommendations, search engines, Web hosting, Internet domains, HTML templates, tools, tips, and more. The Quick Start guide can take you through the process in much

e way I try to do in this book, with a few advantages, of
The site can be updated to reflect changes that occur after
publication, and you can download tools and templates that cannot be delivered in print.

Pop-Up/Pop-Under Affiliate Ads
www.tamingthebeast.net/articles2/pop-under-ads.htm
   This site has a strange name: TamingTheBeast.net. But it includes a page on a type of affiliate advertising you may overlook otherwise. You are probably familiar with pop-up or pop-under ads that appear when you visit certain web sites. You can publish such ads and affiliate fees when they appear. They aren't terribly popular with Web surfers, to say the least. But as a publisher, they can give you an easy way to make some extra money—if you own a web site, that is.

Amazon.com aStores
http://aStore.amazon.com

EARN A FEE aStores

   Throughout this book I recommend Amazon.com's marketplace as a good option for starting out in affiliate advertising. Once you start advertising Amazon.com products on Google, MSN, and other search and content networks, you can consider branching out to open up your own aStore. An aStore is a collection of products taken from Amazon.com's marketplace and selected by you. Each of the product listings is an affiliate advertising link: You earn a fee when a click on one of your listings leads to a purchase.

DISCUSSION GROUPS

ABestWeb Affiliate Marketing Forum
www.abestweb.com
   Discussion forums on this site are remarkably specific. Not only are forums provided for affiliate networks such as Commis-

sion Junction, Linkshare, and ShareASale, but also for individual merchants within those networks. Some of the postings might look like spam, because they are promoting individual sales on products. But these are actually promotions that you can refer to your affiliate ads.

Affiliate Programs Community–Affiliate Message Board and Forum

www.affcommunity.com

Discussions on this site take a different approach from those on ABestWeb. Although there are a few groups that discuss specific affiliate programs or networks, this site provides general discussion. It also gets a far larger number of posts than the forums on ABestWeb. The forum named Newbie Affiliate Questions is a particularly useful resource for beginners who have questions.

Affiliate Marketing Blog

www.affiliatemarketingblog.com

This blog attracts contributions from a group of marketers. Each one starts out a discussion by posting comments on a topic of interest. At the time this is being written, topics include "Google AdWords Secrets," "Website Marketing Design–Effective Content," "Not getting paid!" and more. Readers have the ability to post responses on each of these comments, thus initiating minidiscussions.

EVENTS FOR AFFILIATE MARKETERS *Seminars Conventions*

www.affiliateguide.com/events.html

This page on the AffiliateGuide.com site lists conventions and other events where you can compare notes with other affiliate marketers. In many events, you'll also have the chance to learn about the latest trends in affiliate marketing from experts in the industry.

NEWS AND COMMENTARY ON AFFILIATE MARKETING

The Daily SearchCast

www.webmasterradio.fm/episodes/index.php?showId=30

This "channel" of the Webmaster Radio site is devoted to search engines. Most of the daily broadcasts tend to be about Google. But Yahoo! is also mentioned. The advertising programs offered by both services are occasionally included among the topics being discussed.

Affiliate News and Directories

www.affiliatetip.com/affiliate_newsletter.php

Affiliate marketer Shawn Collins produces a monthly newsletter on his AffiliateTip Web site, AffiliateGuide.com. Regular features include Top 10 Affiliate Programs, which consists of the top 10 for the preceding month, and Affiliate Program News, which lists new and lucrative opportunities for publishers.

Affiliate Guide

www.affiliateguide.com

This is one of the oldest and most respected directories of affiliate programs. The site's home page contains many listings of books related to affiliate advertising, but scroll down the page for a long listing of affiliate programs, many of which offer lucrative payoffs.

CPA Tipline Newsletter

www.cpatipline.com

This is an opt-in e-mail newsletter: Send the publisher your e-mail address and you receive the publication in your inbox on a regular basis. The publication makes money by providing space to advertisers. It also provides value to subscribers by suggesting cost-per-action (CPA) and cost-per-lead programs that are especially profitable.

REFERENCE MATERIALS

Affilipedia

www.affilipedia.com/index.php/Main_Page

This site attempts to create a knowledge base for affiliate marketing that resembles Wikipedia. Affilipedia calls itself "the affiliate marketing encyclopedia." Individual marketers are invited to contribute their own articles and edits to the site. As of this writing, however, only a few articles were presented.

Glossary

The field of online advertising in general, and affiliate marketing in particular, has a language all its own. Many terms are used to describe different payment systems, and many formulas reflect the performance of individual campaigns. The following glossary scratches the surface and gives you the basic terms you need to get started.

Above the fold. A term that originated with newspapers and that referred to a story or ad that appeared on the top half of the printed page where more people would see it. On the Web, this term refers to the first computer screen of Web page content before the user has to scroll down the page.

Ad group. A group of one or more ads promoting the same product or service and sharing the same set of keywords.

AdSense. An advertising program run by the search and content provider Google that enables web site owners to place contextual ads on their content web sites and receive payment for clicks or purchases that result from such placement.

AdWords. An advertising program run by the search and content network Google that allows individuals to place sponsored ads on search results pages and pay for them on a cost-per-click basis.

Affiliate. An individual or company that advertises on behalf of a merchant's products or services. The affiliate receives a commission from the merchant if a referral results in a sale or registration.

Affiliate network. A company that functions as a clearinghouse for affiliate programs and that makes it easy for affiliates to sign up for programs and receive commissions for referrals.

Affiliate program. A program in which companies offer commissions to companies or individuals who advertise for them.

Broad match. A keyword matching type in which an ad is displayed when the keyword appears in a search query, with or without other keywords, in any order and in any combination.

Budget maximum. The maximum amount you are willing to spend on a given campaign.

Campaign. A collection of related ad groups.

Click fraud. A collection of unscrupulous practices, any of which could result in someone unfairly paying for an invalid click.

Click-through rate (CTR). The number of times an ad is clicked on divided by the number of times it appears.

Contextual ads. Ads that are displayed on Web pages according to their relevance to the content of the page. (Also known as *content-match ads*.)

Conversion. The process of converting clicks to commissionable actions.

Conversion rate. A measurement of the rate at which an advertiser converts clicks to sales. If an ad attracts 100 clicks and two people end up making a purchase, the conversion rate is 2 percent.

Cost per click (CPC). This is the cost to you each time someone clicks on one of your ads.

CPM. Cost per thousand impressions, a formula sometimes still used to price conventional banner ads.

Deferred action. Actions that don't take place immediately. If someone clicks on an ad but doesn't make a purchase for a week, that is deferred action.

Destination URL. The URL that a paid search ad actually points to. It is typically the URL of a tracking server that will track and redirect the user to the display URL or to a landing page on the displayed URL's site.

Display URL. The URL that appears in a paid search ad, but not necessarily the exact or immediate destination of the ad.

Earnings per click (EPC). The gross commission earnings, on a per-click basis, of click traffic to an affiliate site. It is calculated using the following formula:

$$\text{Commissions earned} \div \text{total clicks} = \text{EPC}$$

Exact match. A keyword match type that causes an ad to be displayed on a search results page only if the exact keyword or words appear, in the correct order and with no other words, in a search query.

Hit. A request for a file that occurs when a browser visits a Web page.

Keyword. A word or phrase used to locate content through a search site. Keywords are used by individuals to search for content on the Internet. They are also used by advertisers who want their ads to appear in response to a search query for specific keywords.

Keyword list. A compilation of keywords associated with an ad or ad group.

Landing page. The page that appears after someone clicks on an ad.

Negative match. A keyword matching type that, when a negative keyword appears in a search query, causes the associated ad *not* to appear.

Pay per action. An advertising model in which affiliates are paid for certain results, which might include a download, a subscription, a registration, a lead, or other action.

Pay per click (PPC). A system in which an advertiser pays only when an ad is clicked on, rather than for each time it is viewed.

Pay per lead. Commissions program in which the affiliate is paid only when a valid sales lead is generated.

Performance monitoring. The process of monitoring campaigns for the purposes of improving their performance.

Performance tier. A level of advertising performance that, when reached, leads to better commissions.

Phrase match. A keyword match type that causes an ad to be displayed only if the search terms include the exact phrase.

Projected RPC (pRPC). The projected return per click of a campaign, based on the projected performance tier that campaign will reach during the performance period.

Quality score. A ranking used by Google and other search engines to determine ad rank and placement, cost per click, and the minimum bid required for a keyword. The score is based on ad and keyword CTRs, historical performance, and other factors.

Return per click (RPC). The profit (or loss) on a per-click basis of a paid search campaign.

$$\text{Earnings per click} - \text{cost per click} = \text{return} - \text{per click}$$
$$EPC - CPC = RPC$$

Volume. The number of either sales, clicks, items shipped, and so on in a given period.

Index